Cooking with Stored Foods

Carroll Latham & Carlene Tejada

ANOTHER BEST-SELLING VOLUME FROM H.P. BOOKS

Editorial Director: Helen Fisher; Editor: Veronica Durie; Art Director: Don Burton; Book Design: Ken Heiden; Typography: Cindy Coatsworth, Joanne Nociti, Michelle Claridge; Food Stylist: Janet Pittman; Photography: George de Gennaro Studios

Published by H.P. Books, P.O. Box 5367, Tucson, AZ 85703   602/888-2150
ISBN 0-89586-120-8
Library of Congress Catalog Card No. 81-83913
©1981 Fisher Publishing, Inc. Printed in U.S.A.

Cover photo: Festive Ham, page 138; Refrigerated Rolls, page 123; and Freezer Red Raspberry Jam, page 25.

Stocking up on food will add convenience, thrift and security to your life-style.

Convenience—Save time and energy by having food on hand when you need it. Avoid unplanned shopping trips and unexpected dips into your budget.

Thrift—Take advantage of warehouse prices. Buying in bulk or by the case is more economical than buying a single item. In times of rising costs, you will be eating tomorrow at yesterday's prices.

Security—In a financial crisis, stored food is like money in the bank. It will help you through such emergencies as those caused by bad weather, illness or transportation problems.

Storing Is Saving!

With the help of this book, you can dine well using canned, frozen and dried foods.

You can plan dinners for several weeks ahead without dipping into your savings. You will find it easier to cook, entertain and enjoy festive dinners during the holidays because you stocked ingredients for holiday cooking during the year.

As you use this book, you will become acquainted with foods that add flavor, texture and variety to your diet. You will develop new and valuable ways for planning menus and food storage. You will increase your chances of happy survival in a complicated world!

How to Begin

There are several methods of stocking food. The easiest for most people is frequently to buy 2 items for storage when you buy 1 item for current use.

Another method is to investigate warehouses, wholesalers and supermarkets to find where you can get special prices for food bought by the case. Then buy your storage supply gradually or all at once. Be sure you're ready with adequate shelves and freezer space.

Three Rules of Food Storage

Follow these 3 rules to enjoy stored foods.

Store what you eat and eat what you store. Draw from your stored foods every day and replenish them regularly. Do not store foods you and your family are not familiar with. Most people do not adjust easily to new foods.

Use, rotate and store. Do not let containers of food gather in your cupboard corners, on bottom shelves or in back rows. Use a grease pencil to mark the purchase date on cans or boxes, then use the oldest foods first. Rotating foods ensures best flavor and high nutritional content. For information on storage systems that help you rotate foods, see opposite.

Serve at least one fresh food at each meal. This is not as impossible as it sounds. The most obvious solution is a garden. A few carrots or onions grown in a pot on a porch or windowsill can add fresh, crisp enjoyment to meals.

Sprout your own mung beans, alfalfa or wheat, pages 8 and 96. Sprinkle them over salads, vegetables, casseroles and soups. Alfalfa sprouts are also excellent in sandwiches.

Fresh vegetables can be at your fingertips all year with a root cellar, page 4. If you don't have space for a root cellar, follow the directions for storing onions at room temperature, page 16.

Rotating Stored Foods

Rotate stored foods and you'll always be sure of high quality and fine flavor. In general, when you buy new items, push previously purchased ones to the front of the shelf or storage area. Place the new items behind them.

Commercially canned foods must be used within 1 to 2 years. Home-canned products should be used within 1 to 3 years.

Stacked Rotation

Stack canned goods 4 or 5 deep and 2 high on horizontal shelves. For stability, separate stacked cans with a strip of cardboard the width of the cans. Starting at the left, label the shelf in front of each row with **1**, **2**, **3**, **4** and **5**. Remove cans from row **1** until all are used (A). Move all cans in rows **2** through **5** to the left. This will leave row **5** empty (B). Buy enough cans of that food to fill up row **5** (C).

Gravity Rotation

Store round metal cans of food on slanting 8- to 10-inch wide shelves with 1 end 1 to 2 inches higher than the other. Cans placed on the higher end of the shelf roll to the lower end where they are removed; see diagram opposite. Rotation is automatically done for you by gravity.

Storage Systems

Every home contains unused space. Look for cool, dry areas in cupboards, closets, storage rooms, basements, air-conditioned attics, under beds, behind couches, inside furniture, inside walls and behind books on bookshelves. These areas should be clean and dark.

Build shelves for stacked rotation with metal shelving strips and brackets on which boards are placed. Each shelf should have a 1/2- to 1-inch wide strip of wood or metal attached along the outer edge for security.

Wall paneling can be hinged or made to slide to the side, revealing shelves wide enough to hold single rows of cans. Full-size closet doors or cabinet doors with shelves attached will require strong hinges.

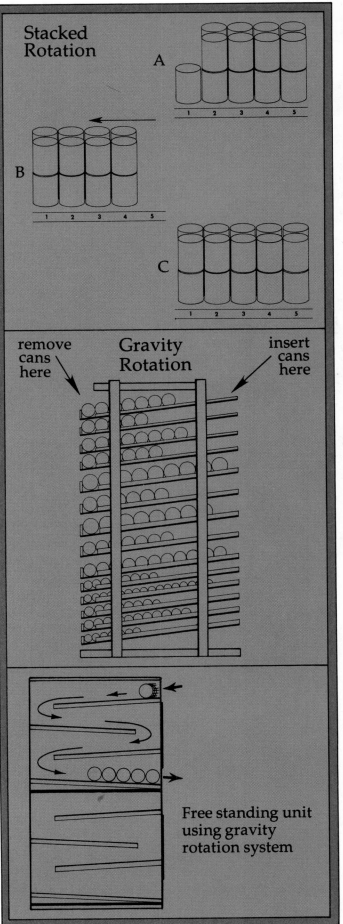

Stacked Rotation

Gravity Rotation

remove cans here

insert cans here

Free standing unit using gravity rotation system

Slanting shelves for gravity rotation should be made with braced shelves, not metal strips and brackets. Brackets interfere with cans as they roll. Distance between the shelves is the diameter of cans placed on each shelf plus 1/4 inch. Attach a 1-1/2-inch by 1/4-inch wooden or metal strip to the outer edge of the shelf to keep cans from rolling off. Attach strips of small half- or quarter-molding as dividers to keep each can on its own track. Plan so the entry points for slanting shelves are near the unloading point, such as in a carport or garage wall. The removal point can be in or close to the kitchen.

Free-standing units using this same gravity rotation system can be placed in closets or other small spaces. Cans are inserted at the top and roll from slanting shelf to slanting shelf; see diagram on page 3.

Make an attractive table by stacking 5-gallon cans of wheat, beans, rice or other bulk storage, in 3 stacks of 2 cans each. Top them with a round, square or rectangular piece of 1-inch plywood and cover with a floor-length cloth.

Large cans can be used to separate shelves holding books or toys.

Root Cellar Storage

Most vegetables store well in a cool, moist cellar, but some require special care. See page 14.

Although basements in centrally heated homes may be too warm and dry, you can adapt a corner for storage. Section off a part of the north or east side of the basement. It should be well-insulated and protected from light. After you've installed shelves, scatter sawdust on the floor and moisten it to increase humidity. Place removable slats on the floor to allow ventilation around foods. Because of the dampness, do not store wheat, rice or beans in this area.

In cool climates, basements in homes without central heating provide excellent storage space. In warmer climates where underground temperatures remain at 72F (22C) all year, basements must be mechanically cooled.

Mounds and pits are inexpensive and vegetables can be stored in them for several months.

For mound storage (A), select a well-drained level area, 3- to 5-feet square. Cover it with 4 to 6 inches of dry straw. Arrange several bushels of root vegetables or cabbages over the straw, bringing them to a peak in the center. Cover with 3 to 4 inches of straw. Cover the straw with 3 to 4 inches of earth, leaving the center peak

uncovered. As the weather gets colder, place more earth and straw over the mound. To remove vegetables, open the peaked area and remove what you need. Carefully cover the area again.

For pit storage (B), dig several holes 3-feet deep and about 4-feet square in well-drained areas. Line them with 4 to 5 inches of dry straw. Layer vegetables with about 1 inch of straw between layers. About 8 inches from the top, cover the vegetables with 2 to 3 inches of straw. Place a canvas or metal covering over the straw. The metal or canvas should cover all but a strip along 1 side wide enough to put your arm down into the pit. Cover the metal or canvas with soil.

Building an insulated outbuilding is a major undertaking, but can be worthwhile if you have your own garden. Ask your State Extension Service or County Extension Agent for *Plan 5948*. Or write to Cooperative Farm Building Plan Exchange and Rural Housing, Building 228, ARC-East, Agricultural Research Service, U.S. Department of Agriculture, Beltsville, MD 20705. Send a self-addressed, stamped envelope.

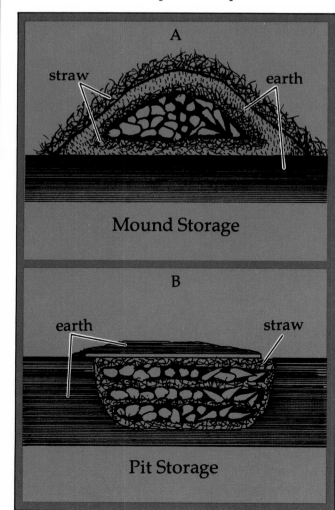

A

straw   earth

Mound Storage

B

earth   straw

Pit Storage

Store-A-Meal

Many recipes in this book can be partially mixed ahead. This is convenient for a camping trip, for quick and easy cooking on moving day and for an emergency storage box.

Read the recipe and the variation to find out which dry ingredients can be mixed in advance. Combine these ingredients in an airtight plastic bag or a container with a tight-fitting lid. Label the container with the date and name of the recipe as well as the page number the recipe is on. Store in a cool, dry place in a labeled box or plastic bag with whatever canned or packaged foods are needed. Include a can opener, a knife and a mixing spoon. If legumes, dried vegetables, rice, pasta or any powdered ingredients are to be added separately, measure the amounts and store them in separate airtight containers.

Store-a-Meal Ideas

Take the ingredients to make Campers' Beef & Barley Stew, page 82, on a camping trip. Tuck in a container of Tantalizing Trail Mix, page 32.

On a hectic moving day, have ready the ingredients for Campers' Brown Rice & Raisins, page 60, Campers' Split Peas Punjabi-Style, page 65, and Campers' Tartlets, page 145.

Keep the ingredients for Campers' Brunswick Stew, page 70, in your emergency storage box. A supply of Easy Muffins, page 127, and Fudge Cookies, page 155, in your freezer will round out the meal.

Power Outage

Occasionally households or entire communities experience loss of electric power. If you presently rely on a freezer for food storage, it's a good idea to enlarge your storage to include canned and dried items.

Refrigerators & Freezers

If possible, don't open your refrigerator or freezer until power is restored. If the freezer is not opened, food will stay frozen for 1 to 3 days. The smaller the amount of food in the freezer, the shorter the time food will stay frozen.

Stoves & Ovens

Large, heavy, covered pans or Dutch ovens can be used in fireplaces or can be placed in the hot coals of an outdoor fire. Shovel more hot coals over the top of the pot to make an oven.

Instructions for making a solar oven or a reflector oven can be obtained from a library, your County Extension Agent or from boy-scout manuals.

It is easy to make a *buddy burner* from flat tuna or pineapple cans. Cut corrugated cardboard as wide as the can is high, cutting across the corrugated strips. Coil the cardboard tightly inside the can. Pour melted paraffin or candle-wax over and between the coils until the can is full. **Use extreme caution when handling hot paraffin or candle-wax.** After the wax or paraffin has hardened, light the coils by placing several burning matches across the top. Buddy burners should be placed inside a *can-stove,* see below, or between rocks so heat is directed up to a pan placed over the burner.

A small outdoor can-stove can be made from a number-10 can or a 46-ounce juice can. On the open end, cut out a piece of metal about 3 inches high and 3 to 4 inches long. On the closed end of the can, use a punch can-opener to make holes around the side at about 3-inch intervals. Through the large hole, insert a lighted buddy burner, or twisted paper and sticks to make a fire. Some foods such as bacon and eggs can be cooked directly on the surface of the can-stove. Pans or skillets can also be used on the stove.

Construct a simple oven by placing another, slightly smaller can on top of your can-stove. Biscuits, cakes and quick breads can be baked in these makeshift ovens.

How to Make a Buddy Burner

Coil corrugated-cardboard strips tightly inside cans. Pour melted candle-wax or paraffin over and between cardboard coils until the can is full.

How to Make a Can-Stove

Cut a piece of metal from the open end of a number-10 can or 46-ounce juice can. Punch holes around top of closed end. Insert lighted buddy burner.

Water Emergencies

The Federal Emergency Management Agency recommends storing 14 gallons of water per person for drinking and food preparation. This is a 2-week supply. Store another 7 gallons per person for bathing, brushing teeth and washing dishes.

Water stored for emergencies must be clean. Use clean plastic or glass jugs, or jars with tight-fitting lids. Water stored in metal containers may develop a metallic taste.

If you doubt the purity of stored water, boil it for 10 minutes before using. Or for every gallon of water, add 4 water purification tablets, 12 drops of tincture of iodine, or 8 drops of chlorine bleach that contains hypochlorite as its *only* active ingredient. Add a few grains of salt to stored water to take away the bland taste.

Foods You Need To Know About

Bacon

Bacon is one of the most enticing flavorings. It is absolutely essential for some recipes.

Freezing Bacon: Buy packages of ends and pieces. Divide the bacon into 1/4-pound portions. Wrap each portion in freezer wrap. Label the packages with date and contents before freezing. If you put the packages of bacon in a large freezer bag or container, they won't disappear in the corners of your freezer. Use a portion of bacon to season a pot of beans, a stew or a casserole. Cook and crumble bacon to make bacon omelets or bacon muffins. Or sprinkle it on top of a salad or casserole.

Canned Bacon: Store at least 2 or 3 cans of bacon. It's easy to store and practical if you're short of freezer space. Canned bacon may be available in supermarket meat cases or in some gourmet shops. To use, follow the directions on the can.

How to Store Water

Store water in clean plastic or glass containers with tight-fitting lids. To purify water, use water purification tablets, tincture of iodine, or chlorine bleach containing hypochlorite as its only active ingredient.

How to Freeze Bacon

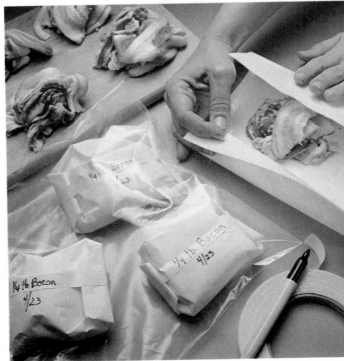

Divide bacon ends and pieces into 1/4-pound portions. Wrap each portion in freezer wrap and label. Place packages in a large freezer container or bag and freeze.

Bean Curd

Made from soybeans, bean curd, or *tofu*, is extremely high in protein.

Diced bean curd can be sprinkled on salads, stirred into soups or fried in skillet dishes. Look for recipes using bean curd in *Chinese Cookery*, published by HPBooks.

Freezing Bean Curd: You can freeze bean curd in small freezer containers. Be sure there is no water in the container. To thaw frozen bean curd, add a little water to the container and let it stand a few hours in the refrigerator.

How to Make Bean Curd

Sort and rinse 1 cup of dried soybeans. Place in a large bowl and add water to cover. Soak soybeans 10 to 12 hours. Drain and rinse the soybeans. Mix 4 teaspoons of cider vinegar with 1/2 cup of water and set the mixture aside.

Place a colander in a medium saucepan. Line the colander with 2 layers of cheesecloth. Process 1 cup of soybeans in a blender with 3/4 cup of fresh water until smooth. Pour the mixture into the lined colander. Repeat with remaining soybeans, 1 cup at a time, adding 3/4 cup of fresh water to each cup of soybeans. Bring the ends of the cheesecloth together and twist to close. Hold the twisted ends with 1 hand and squeeze the soybean liquid through the cheesecloth into the saucepan with your other hand. Squeeze until all liquid is removed. Discard the cheesecloth and the paste it contains.

Bring the soybean liquid to a boil over medium-low heat, stirring occasionally. Remove from heat and add vinegar mixture, stirring 3 or 4 times in a single direction only. Let the mixture stand about 5 minutes until curds form. Line a flat-bottom colander or other perforated container with 2 layers of cheesecloth. Pour the soy curds into the colander. Fold the cheesecloth ends over the curds. Place a plate or other flat object on top. Place a heavy object such as a gallon jug full of water on top of the plate. Let it stand 15 minutes.

Remove the heavy object and plate. Unfold the cheesecloth. Place a container upside down over the colander. Invert the colander and container. Remove the colander and cheesecloth. Cut bean curd into pieces 2 to 3 inches square. Use it immediately or pour cold water over it to cover. Close the container and refrigerate it. Bean curd will keep 1 to 2 weeks if you change the water daily.

Beans, dried

See Rice, Pasta & Beans, page 58.

Bean Sprouts

Although most legumes can be sprouted, mung beans are the most popular for sprouting at home. Bean sprouts are rich in vitamins A and C. They add crispness to salads, soups and vegetables. Stir-fry them with onions, cabbage and frozen peas or pea pods or sauté them with scrambled eggs. For more ways to use bean sprouts, see *Bean Cookery* and *Chinese Cookery*. Both books are published by HPBooks.

How to Sprout Mung Beans

Sort and rinse 3/4 cup of dried beans. Place in a large bowl and add water to cover. Soak beans 10 to 12 hours. Drain and rinse the beans. Place the soaked beans in a jar and cover them with water. Cover the jar opening with cheesecloth and secure it with a rubber band or string (A). Hold the jar upside down to drain out all the water. Then place the jar on its side or upside down on a wire cooling rack. Cover the jar with a cloth towel to protect the beans from light, but do not cover the opening of the jar (B). Let stand at room temperature. You do not have to remove the cheesecloth cover to rinse the beans. Run water directly through the cheesecloth and turn the jar upside down to drain the beans. Do this twice a day. In 3 to 5 days, when the sprouts are 1 to 2 inches long, give them a final rinse and refrigerate them in a covered container. They will stay fresh 4 to 7 days.

How to Sprout Mung Beans

A

B

Butter & Margarine

Butter and margarine can be refrigerated for several weeks and frozen for several months.

Butter-Flavor Granules: Packages are available in most supermarkets. They can be stored at room temperature and require only hot water to develop the flavor of melted butter. They can also be mixed with other liquids or vegetable oil. The granules can be used to flavor vegetables, pasta, soups and sauces. Be sure the food contains sufficient liquid to dissolve the granules.

Because butter-flavor granules contain no fat, they cannot be used for sautéing or frying.

Clarified Butter: If you have no way to freeze or refrigerate butter or margarine, you can rely on clarified butter, which is butter with the milk solids removed. Without milk solids, butter will keep at room temperature for a month or longer. It can be refrigerated for several months.

To make clarified butter, melt butter in a heavy pan over low heat. Remove the pan from the heat. As the melted butter cools, the milk solids sink to the bottom, leaving a layer of clear butter on top. Carefully spoon the clear layer into a container with a tight-fitting lid. If you suspect your clarified butter contains even a drop of milk solids, it's best to refrigerate it.

Powdered Butter: You can buy powdered butter in cans from retailers selling dehydrated foods and food-storage programs. Look in the yellow pages of your phone book under *Dehydrated Foods.*

Butter powder can be reconstituted to make a butter spread. It can also be used to flavor sauces and soups. Butter powder should be stored at room temperature.

Cabbage

Instructions for storing cabbage in a root cellar are on pages 4 and 14.

Freezing Cabbage: Shred or chop cabbage and place in a freezer bag. Label and place in the freezer. Freezing and thawing makes cabbage limp because of its high water content. But it will still be a boon when you're creating a wholesome satisfying soup. Just reach in the bag and drop a handful or two of cabbage in the soup a few minutes before serving it.

How to Freeze Cabbage

Shred or chop cabbage and place in a freezer bag. Label, close tightly and place in the freezer.

Carrots

Instructions for storing root vegetables such as carrots in a root cellar are on pages 4 and 14.

Drying Carrots: You can dry carrot shreds in your oven. Set the oven thermostat at warm or the lowest setting. Place an oven thermometer in the oven. Preheat the oven until the oven thermometer registers 130F (55C). While the oven is heating, shred several carrots on the coarsest side of your grater. Spread the carrot shreds in a single layer on 1 or 2 ungreased baking sheets. Place the baking sheets in the warm oven. Close the oven door. You may have to turn the oven on and off several times to maintain the temperature at 130F (55C). The carrots will dry in 2 to 3 hours.

If you live in a dry, sunny climate, dry carrot shreds on baking sheets outdoors in a sheltered area. Turn them often with a spatula so they'll dry evenly. You may have to place a window screen or fine nylon mesh over the baking sheets to protect the carrot shreds from insects and breezes.

If you have a microwave oven, shred a carrot onto a paper towel. Cover the shreds with another paper towel and put them in the microwave oven set on high. Watch carefully because the shreds will be dry in 5 to 10 minutes.

Store carrot flakes in small airtight containers in a dark cupboard.

Freezing Carrots: Shred carrots and divide them among small containers or sandwich bags, placing about 1/3 cup in each container. Close tightly and label each container. Drop all the containers in a freezer bag. Secure the bag with a twist tie and store in your freezer.

After carrot shreds thaw, they will be a little watery. If you intend to use the carrots raw, let them stand uncovered for 30 minutes to 1 hour before using. If the carrots will be cooked in a stew or soup, they can be added immediately.

How to Freeze Carrots

Shred carrots and place in freezer bags or small containers. Label, close tightly and place in the freezer.

Cheese

Depending on the kind of cheese, it can be refrigerated from 2 weeks to 6 months. Soft natural cheeses keep about 2 weeks in the refrigerator. Hard cheeses can be refrigerated 6 months or longer. To keep hard cheese from becoming moldy, lightly dampen a piece of cheesecloth with white distilled vinegar. Wrap the cheese in the vinegar cloth and place in a plastic bag. Secure the bag with a twist tie and refrigerate.

Freezing Cheese: Cut hard cheese into 1/2- to 1-pound pieces. Wrap each piece in freezer wrap before freezing. If you expect to keep the cheese frozen for a long time, overwrap it in aluminum foil or in a freezer bag. Cheese can be grated and then frozen in freezer bags or containers.

Thaw cheese in the refrigerator and use it as soon as possible. Thawed frozen cheese may crumble when you cut it. The surface may be a little discolored from moisture, but this will not change the flavor.

Soft cheeses do not freeze as well as hard cheeses. The texture of some will change drastically. Cottage cheese becomes grainy and cream cheese will be dry and less smooth. This does not affect their use in cooking.

Powdered Cheese: You can buy Cheddar cheese powder in cans from retailers selling dehydrated foods and food-storage programs. Look in the yellow pages of your phone book under *Dehydrated Foods.*

Cheese powder can be stored at room temperature. Use it dry or mix it with liquid or oil. Follow the package directions. The texture and consistency of the powder, dry or reconstituted, does not resemble fresh cheese, but it does add cheese flavor.

Citrus Fruits

Freeze several bags of whole lemons, limes and oranges so you'll always have fruit wedges and slices for garnishing platters, salads and cold drinks.

Freezing Citrus Fruits: Wash and thoroughly dry the fresh fruit. Place fruit in a freezer bag. Remove as much air as possible from the bag by sucking it out with a straw or squeezing it out. Close the bag with a twist tie. Label and freeze. Frozen lemons, limes, oranges and grapefruit will keep in your freezer for 6 months to a year. Slice them while they are frozen or thaw them at room temperature 1-1/2 to 3 hours or in the refrigerator overnight. Use frozen citrus fruits immediately after thawing.

How to Freeze Citrus Fruit

Place washed fruit in a freezer bag. Remove as much air as possible from bag by sucking it out with a straw or squeezing it out. Close bag with a twist tie. Label and place in the freezer.

Citrus Peel

You can buy sweetened lemon peel and orange peel granules in supermarkets. Look for them in the spice section.

Drying Citrus Peel: Set the oven thermostat at warm or the lowest setting. Place an oven thermometer in the oven. Preheat the oven until the thermometer registers 130F (55C). While the oven is heating, use a vegetable peeler to strip the thin outer peel from the fruit. Be careful not to include the bitter white portion under the outer skin. Arrange the citrus strips in a single layer on a wire cooling rack. Place the cooling rack in the warm oven. Close the oven door. You may have to turn the oven on and off several times to maintain the temperature between 120F and 130F (50C and 55C). Too high temperature may destroy the flavor of the oil in the peel. The peel will be dry and crisp after 2 to 3 hours. Break peel into convenient lengths and store in a small container. Store it in a cool, dry, dark cupboard. Dried citrus peel will keep for at least 9 months.

Before using, grind dried peel in a blender or food processor or crush between pieces of waxed paper with a rolling pin.

Freezing Citrus Peel: Prepare the peel as for drying. Spread the strips of peel in a single layer on a baking sheet. Place uncovered in the freezer for 4 to 6 hours until the strips are stiff. Place peel in small freezer containers or small plastic bags. Label containers. Drop containers into a large freezer bag. Secure the bag with a twist tie and store in your freezer for 4 to 6 months.

Grind peel while frozen in the same way as dried peel.

You can also grate peel off the fresh fruit and store it in small freezer containers.

Cream

Freezing Cream: Frozen cream does not whip well. If you want a store of whipped cream, whip it first and add sugar as desired. Place a piece of waxed paper on a baking sheet. Drop whipped cream by dollops or pipe it onto waxed paper. Leave it uncovered in the freezer only until the mounds are frozen. Remove the frozen mounds from the waxed paper. Pack them into a freezer container in layers with a piece of waxed paper between each layer. Cover the container tightly. Label and store in the freezer for up to 2 weeks.

To serve the whipped-cream mounds, arrange frozen mounds on top of cakes and desserts. Let the cake or dessert stand at room temperature a few minutes before serving.

Eggs

Fresh eggs can be stored 4 to 5 weeks in the refrigerator if you leave them in the carton. You can also store whole frozen eggs, separated frozen eggs, frozen egg substitutes, fresh eggs in water glass or dried eggs.

Frozen eggs, frozen egg substitutes and dried eggs should be used only in foods that are to be cooked. Uncooked, unpasteurized eggs provide a perfect environment for some bacteria. If you need raw eggs for eggnog or salad dressing, use only very fresh eggs or be sure the form of eggs you use is labeled *pasteurized*.

Freezing Eggs: Rinse the egg in cold water before cracking to prevent dirt or dust on the shell from falling into the egg.

Frozen whole mixed eggs contain both the yolk and the white. Crack the eggs into a bowl. Mix them thoroughly but gently without beating in any air. When the eggs are mixed, measure them. For baking, add sugar or corn syrup. For scrambled eggs, omelets or as a main dish ingredient, add salt. Stir in 3/4 teaspoon sugar or corn syrup or 1/4 teaspoon salt for each 1/2 cup of mixed eggs. Salt or sweetening will keep the eggs free from lumps through the freezing and thawing processes.

Lightly oil muffin cups with a paper towel moistened with vegetable oil. Pour 3 tablespoons of egg mixture—the equivalent of 1 whole egg—into each oiled muffin cup. Cover the muffin cups with plastic wrap and place in the freezer for 1 to 2 hours. When the eggs are frozen, they should slip easily out of the muffin cups. If they do not, dip the bottom of the cups in warm water. Turn the eggs into a freezer container. Label with the date and indicate whether the eggs are sweetened or salted. Cover tightly and store in your freezer. Remove the number of eggs you need from the freezer a few hours in advance. Thaw them in the refrigerator in a covered container. If they are not thawed when you are ready to use them, place the container in a bowl of warm water.

If you expect to use a large number of mixed eggs at a certain time, freeze them together in a large freezer container. Indicate the number of eggs on the label. This is helpful for holiday baking.

Whole mixed eggs can be stored in your freezer for 9 months.

Egg yolks to be frozen separately should be mixed slightly, but not beaten. Treat them as mixed whole eggs, adding 1-1/2 teaspoons of sugar or corn syrup or 1/4 teaspoon of salt to each 1/2 cup of mixed egg yolks. Freeze large quantities in a single container or freeze smaller amounts in an ice-cube tray. One tablespoon equals 1 egg yolk. To be sure you have 1 egg yolk to 1 cube, mix the yolks in a measuring cup. There are 16 tablespoons in 1 cup. If you have 1/2 cup of yolks, divide them equally among 8 cube sections.

Egg yolks can be stored in your freezer for 9 months.

Egg whites can be frozen in ice-cube trays as well as in bulk. One egg white equals 1-1/2 tablespoons. The number of egg whites you freeze together depends on your cooking needs. Do not beat egg whites before freezing them. Thawed frozen egg whites can be stiffly beaten as easily as fresh egg whites.

Frozen egg whites can be stored in your freezer for 9 to 12 months.

Whole unmixed eggs are perfect for fried and poached eggs. Lightly oil muffin cups with a paper towel dipped in vegetable oil. Break eggs into the muffin cups without breaking the yolks, placing 1 egg in each cup. Cover muffin cups with plastic wrap and place in the freezer until the eggs are frozen, 1 to 2 hours. If the eggs do not slip out of the cups easily, dip the bottom of the cups in warm water. Remove the eggs and place them in a freezer container. Close tightly and store in your freezer. Remove the number of eggs you need from the freezer a few hours in advance. Thaw them in the refrigerator in a covered container. Eggs to be used for breakfast can be thawed in the refrigerator overnight.

Do not use whole frozen eggs for scrambled eggs, omelets, quiches or in other cooked or baked dishes requiring mixed eggs. Unless yolks have a stabilizer such as salt, sugar or corn syrup added, they will not return to their original consistency when thawed and will not beat into a smooth mixture.

Egg Equivalents for Home-Frozen Eggs
1 cup mixed whole eggs = 5 eggs
1 tablespoon egg yolk = 1 egg yolk
1-1/2 to 2 tablespoons egg white = 1 egg white
3 tablespoons mixed whole egg = 1 egg
Medium-size eggs are used throughout this book.

Frozen Egg Substitutes: The most common frozen egg substitutes are those based on the original egg. Yolks are removed from whole eggs and soy or milk protein is mixed with the egg whites before they are processed further. Frozen egg substitutes can be used whenever beaten eggs are required. They can be stored in your freezer 6 months to 1 year.

Your own frozen fresh eggs may be 2 to 3 times less expensive than frozen substitutes.

Eggs in Water Glass: Storing eggs in water glass—sodium silicate—is a technique that was used decades ago. Sodium silicate is sold in drugstores. It is a sealing agent so must be discarded where it won't clog pipes.

You will need a large jar or crock with a cover. To prevent breakage, place a long metal ladle or spatula in the container. Then pour in boiling water to clean the container. Pour out the water and remove the ladle or spatula. Boil and cool several cups of water. For every 3 to 4 cups of water, use 1/3 cup of sodium silicate. Measure

How to Store Eggs in Water Glass

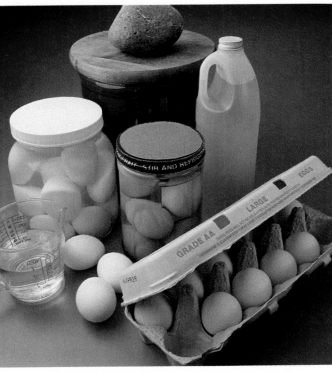

Pour a solution of sodium silicate and water into a large jar or crock until it is half full. Lower eggs into the solution. Cover and label the container. Store in a cool place.

the cooled water into the container until it is about half full, then stir in the sodium silicate. Rinse the eggs to remove any dirt. Use a long spoon to lower them carefully into the solution. The solution should cover the eggs by about 2 inches. Cover the container, label it and store it in a cool place.

Eggs in water glass will keep well for several weeks. After a month or so, the eggs may be slightly watery and won't separate easily. However, the eggs will be fine for baking or scrambling. The longer eggs are stored in water glass at room temperature, the more watery they become. They may be used until they have an unpleasant smell. We have kept eggs as long as 4 months in water glass at room temperature.

If eggs in water glass are refrigerated or kept in a cold storage area, they can be stored for a year. The yolks and whites of these eggs can be more easily separated than those kept at room temperature. Egg whites of refrigerated water-glass eggs will whip to stiff peaks as satisfactorily as those from fresh eggs.

When you are ready to use an egg, choose a container with the earliest date. Reach into the solution with your hand. The egg should be rinsed before breaking it and you can rinse your hand at the same time. Crack the egg into a small bowl or cup. Smell it. If it doesn't have an offensive odor, go ahead and use it.

If an egg should break in the water-glass solution, don't use that egg. The remaining eggs will still be usable, even though the solution itself may develop an unpleasant smell. Remove the eggs from the solution. Store them in the refrigerator and use them as soon as possible.

A practical way to organize eggs stored in water glass is in a number of large wide-mouth jars. We use 2-pound peanut butter jars. They hold 7 medium eggs with some head room.

If your main interest in food storage is to have food on hand for baking during winter holidays, start putting up eggs in water glass before Halloween. You'll be amazed how convenient it is to have those eggs ready when you start baking.

Dried Eggs: Freeze-dried and dehydrated egg solids are easy to use. Most dried-egg products are nitrogen packed, but different methods leave varying amounts of oxygen in the containers. Ask your dealer about residual oxygen. The presence of oxygen will reduce the storage time.

Compare brands and buy the one with the lowest amount.

To combat heat and moisture, store dried eggs in a cool, dry place, preferably 45F to 65F (5C to 20C). They don't need refrigeration. Keep the oxygen content down by keeping the container tightly covered except to spoon out amounts needed for cooking. Do not pour from the container or stir the dried eggs. This will incorporate oxygen.

Most dried eggs are pasteurized. Read labels before you buy. **If they are not pasteurized, don't taste the product made with them until after the food has been cooked.** Cooked products are perfectly safe.

Generally, 1 cup dried whole eggs is equal to 6 fresh large eggs. You can buy dried eggs in 1-pound cans or in 6-1/2- to 6-3/4-pound cans.

You can also buy dried egg yolk solids, dried egg white solids and dried egg mix that may contain dried butter solids, corn oil, salt and coloring. Dried egg whites are as easy to use as fresh egg whites and sometimes yield a greater volume when beaten.

Add dried eggs to baked products by stirring or sifting them into other dry ingredients. Add liquid needed to reconstitute them to other liquids called for in the recipe.

Fish & Seafood

See Chicken & Fish, page 69.

Fruits & Vegetables

Also see Citrus Fruits, page 11.

You can store fruit and vegetables in 4 forms: frozen, canned, dried and fresh in a root cellar, page 4.

Drying fresh fruits and vegetables when you have your own garden has economical advantages. Dried food is expensive and usually contains sugar, salt, preservatives and other ingredients. If you dry your own, you can control the amount of these added ingredients. See *How To Dry Foods*, published by HPBooks.

Dried chopped vegetables, or vegetable flakes, are indispensable. They are an inexpensive way to add flavor to stews, casseroles, sauces and dressings. Some of the most common dried chopped vegetables available in supermarkets are onion, celery and bell peppers. Dried onions are available minced, which is a smaller cut than chopped. Purchase 3 or 4 large containers of each kind of dried chopped vegetable. You will use them by the spoonful. The difference they make in richer, fuller flavor will be worth every penny. See page 9 for how to dry carrots.

Root Cellar Cautions

Some fruits and vegetables emit a gas called *ethylene* which is harmful to other produce. It may cause rapid ripening, spoilage or unpleasant flavors. Avoid storing apples or pears with cabbage, carrots, celery, onions or potatoes. Celery should not be stored with carrots or onions. The USDA recommends that onions, potatoes, nuts, apples, pears and citrus fruits each be stored separately. Pears and apples develop an unpleasant flavor when stored with potatoes. Diseased tissues also produce this gas. Any vegetable that shows signs of decay should immediately be removed from the storage area. There is no danger to humans from ethylene.

Garlic

Garlic is available powdered or dried minced. Fresh garlic can be stored in vegetable oil. Separate and peel each garlic clove. Put the peeled cloves in a small jar with a tight-fitting lid. Pour in vegetable oil to cover the garlic. Cover tightly. Garlic in oil can be refrigerated for 6 months to 1 year. Oil which has been used for storing garlic is a flavorful addition to salad dressings.

In general, 1 medium garlic clove equals 1/8 teaspoon garlic powder or dried minced garlic.

Grains

Many grains can be ground into flour and used as cereal or to thicken soups. Some can be sprouted, see page 96. If you like to include barley or millet in soups, store 3 to 5 pounds of each. Leave them in their original containers and place them in large containers with tight-fitting lids. Rolled oats may be emptied from their containers into firm plastic containers. Rolled oats can be used as they are or ground into flour and used in home-baked breads. Information on wheat is on pages 94 and 95.

Legumes

See Rice, Pasta & Beans, page 58, and *Bean Cookery*, published by HPBooks.

Lemon Juice & Lime Juice

Citrus juices add fresh and tangy flavor to salads, vegetables and soups. You can buy both reconstituted lemon juice and lime juice in bottles and in squeeze containers. These reconstituted juices do not have to be refrigerated until they have been opened and then will keep several months in your refrigerator.

Frozen reconstituted lemon juice can be purchased. Once thawed, it will keep 2 months or longer in your refrigerator.

Lemons & Limes

See Citrus Fruits, page 11.

Meat

See Meat, page 81.

Milk

Dry Milk: You can buy instant non-fat dry milk powder in most supermarkets. Follow the package directions for mixing. When cooking with dry milk, reconstitute it with liquid drained from cooked or canned vegetables and fruits.

Non-instant non-fat dry milk powder is available from most dairies and warehouse outlets. It costs less than the instant variety, but is harder to reconstitute. Combine about 1-1/2 cups non-instant milk powder and 3 to 4 cups water in a blender. Process until the mixture is smooth, scraping all of the milk powder from the sides of the blender. Pour into a 2-quart pitcher. Slowly stir in enough water to fill the pitcher.

If the thinness of reconstituted non-fat dry milk doesn't appeal to you, stir in a little extra dry milk powder, evaporated milk or whole milk.

Dry milk that has not been reconstituted can be kept at room temperature in a tightly covered container for 1 year or longer. Reconstituted dry milk must be refrigerated and will keep several days, but the flavor is best if the milk is cold and is used within 12 hours after making.

Yogurt can be made using reconstituted dry milk. See How to Make Yogurt, page 18.

You may be able to find non-instant dry whole-milk powder in health-food stores, through warehouse outlets, dehydrated-food distributors or your local dairy. Because it contains fat, whole-milk powder will spoil rapidly unless the opened container is covered tightly and refrigerated.

Fresh Milk: For short-term storage, fresh homogenized milk can be frozen in its own unopened waxed containers. It must stand about 48 hours in the refrigerator to thaw completely. Thawing in cold storage helps milk stay fresher longer. If it has been frozen for a long time, the milk may separate. Frozen milk that has not been homogenized will separate as it thaws and the lumps will remain no matter how well you mix it. The suggested storage time for frozen whole milk is 1 to 3 months.

If you want to stretch whole milk or lower its fat content, mix in an equal amount of reconstituted non-fat dry milk.

Evaporated Milk: Equal amounts of water and evaporated milk can be substituted for whole milk. A few ounces of evaporated milk added to a quart of reconstituted non-fat dry milk adds creaminess and body.

Invert cans of evaporated milk every month to keep the milk solids from settling to the bottom. Or lay the cans on slanting shelves. Gravity rotation does the turning for you. Before opening a can of evaporated milk, shake it well or the milk may be lumpy. It is usable unless it has an unpleasant smell. Mix it with a fork or whisk to break up the lumps. Six months is the suggested storage time for unopened cans of evaporated milk. Opened cans of evaporated milk will keep several days in your refrigerator.

Undiluted evaporated milk can often be used as a substitute for cream in cream sauces, cream soups and chowders.

Sweetened Condensed Milk: The process for canning sweetened condensed milk includes adding sugar to milk and removing about half the water content. The cans should be inverted every 2 weeks to prevent the milk solids from settling. Before opening a can of condensed milk, shake it well. Six months is the suggested storage time for unopened cans. Sweetened condensed milk may change color or become lumpy. It is usable unless it has an unpleasant smell. Mix it with a fork or whisk to break up lumps.

Nuts

Freezing Nuts: Freeze shelled unsalted nuts in their own sealed bags or in an airtight container. They will keep from 6 months to 1 year, depending on the age, condition and type of nuts. Whole nuts keep better for long storage than chopped or broken nuts.

To use frozen nuts, remove the amount you need from the container. Let whole nuts stand about 30 minutes to thaw completely. Broken, chopped and slivered nuts will thaw in less time.

Keep salted nuts frozen only 3 to 4 months. They become rancid sooner than unsalted nuts.

Vacuum-Packed Nuts: Unopened containers should be used within 6 months to 1 year. Keep them at room temperature, preferably in a cool, dry place. Refrigerate them once the can is opened.

Unshelled Nuts: These store well for up to 6 months in a cool, dry place. Pour them into strong mesh bags. Hang the bags from the ceiling in a store room. Or, place the nuts in perforated containers to allow air to circulate around them.

Onions

Dried chopped or minced onions can often be substituted for fresh onions, but there are recipes in which fresh onions should be used.

Try growing your own. Onions are easy to care for and can be grown in large pots on a porch or patio.

Fresh onions from your garden must be partially dried before long-term storage. After they are harvested, cut off the tops. Spread the onions in a cool, dry and airy place. The more air allowed to circulate around each onion, the less chance there will be of spoilage. When the outer layers of the onions are dry and tissue-like, the onions will resemble those you buy in the supermarket. They are then ready for storage.

Stored correctly, onions will keep several months. Wrap each onion tightly in a piece of aluminum foil, being sure the onion is completely covered and the foil is sealed. Store the wrapped onions in a box, crate or basket in a cool, dry, well-ventilated place such as an attic or basement. The storage area should have a constant temperature. If the temperature fluctuates, moisture that collects under the foil may cause the onions to spoil. Date each basket or box and use from the container with the earliest date first. Most onions will keep 6 months or longer.

The cooler and drier the storage area, the longer the onions will keep. Onions can also be stored in a root cellar, pages 4 and 14.

Dried chopped or minced onion or dried onion flakes can be bought in supermarkets. If only the flavor of onion is required, use onion powder. This is especially useful for making sauces, cream soups and salad dressings.

Freezing Onions: Chop fresh onions and freeze them in a freezer bag secured with a twist tie. When you need onion for soup, stew or to sauté with meat or a vegetable, drop in a handful of chopped frozen onion. Frozen onions are not crisp when thawed so you may prefer not to use them raw.

How to Store Onions

Wrap whole onions in aluminum foil and store in a cool, dry place. For freezing, place chopped onions in a freezer bag. Label, close tightly and place in the freezer.

Orange Peel, Dried

See Citrus Peel, page 11.

Oranges

See Citrus Fruits, page 11.

Pasta

See Rice, Pasta & Beans, page 58, and *Pasta Cookery*, published by HPBooks.

Peanut Butter

One of the most delicious, nutritious and satisfying foods you can store is peanut butter. It will keep on a cool, dark shelf for 6 months or longer and in your refrigerator for over 1 year. Creamy peanut butter stores better than crunchy peanut butter.

Old-fashioned peanut butter is not hydrogenated and may contain few or no additives. After long storage, it separates into an oily layer at the top and a solid layer at the bottom. It can usually be mixed but it takes a firm utensil and a strong hand to do it. For long storage, old-fashioned peanut butter will keep best in the refrigerator.

Peas, dried

See Rice, Pasta & Beans, page 58.

Potatoes

Fresh potatoes can be stored in a root cellar, pages 4 and 14. If you don't have a root cellar, keep potatoes in vented boxes or baskets in a cool, dry garage or basement. Potatoes can be stored this way for 3 to 4 months. If your garage is unheated in the winter, cover the potatoes with a blanket. If it gets extremely cold, place the potatoes in a Styrofoam cooler or box and cover the box with its lid and a blanket.

Canned Potatoes: These are especially useful because they are already peeled and cooked. Use them in salads, soups and chowders.

Instant Potato Flakes: Store for a year or more in a cool, dry place.

Poultry

See Chicken & Fish, page 69.

Rice

See Rice, Pasta & Beans, page 58.

Seafood

See Chicken & Fish, page 69.

Sweeteners

Sweeteners can be stored for years, but they do need some special considerations.

White Granulated Sugar: White sugar must be kept dry. Store it in containers with tight-fitting lids. Brown sugar may be substituted for white sugar, but it may change the color and flavor of the finished dish.

Brown Sugar: Keep in containers with tight-fitting lids. Unlike white sugar, it should be kept moist or it will harden. Put a piece of fresh bread in each container and the sugar will stay moist. If the sugar has already hardened, add the bread and the sugar will soften after a few days. Replace the bread as it dries out.

Corn Syrup: You can use corn syrup to replace sugar, measure for measure, in quick breads and yeast breads. It can replace half the sugar in fruit breads. In most other recipes, you can replace a fourth of the sugar without changing amounts of other ingredients. If the syrup crystalizes after long storage, place the container in a pan of hot water to melt the crystals.

Honey: You can use honey to replace sugar in the same proportions as corn syrup. For complete success in cooking with honey, use recipes that have been especially developed for its use. Store honey in 1-quart to 1-gallon glass or plastic airtight containers to preserve its flavor and color. To melt honey crystals, stand the container of honey in a pan of hot water. Do not apply heat directly to the container. Do not add water to honey when it will be stored. Water causes the honey to ferment. The Honey Association recommends that infants under 1 year old should not be given honey because it is a raw product and may contain bacteria.

Powdered Sugar: Keep powdered sugar dry and store in containers with tight-fitting lids.

Textured Vegetable Protein (TVP)

Imitation bacon bits are a form of Textured Vegetable Protein. Most forms of TVP must be reconstituted, but bacon bits are meant to be used as they are.

TVP is a vegetable protein made from soybeans but its texture is similar to meat. When used with meat, TVP absorbs the flavor and cannot be distinguished from the meat.

Reconstitute TVP granules with equal amounts of liquid. Broth is best because it gives flavor to TVP. Let the mixture stand about 15 minutes. Then stir it into stews and skillet dishes during the last few minutes of cooking. See the variation for Skillet Supper, page 64.

When adding reconstituted TVP to mixtures for meat loaves, meatballs or hamburger patties, increase the liquid called for by one-third. Then let the meat mixture stand for a few minutes. If it seems dry, add another 1/2 cup of liquid.

Store TVP in airtight containers in a cool, dry place. It will keep about 1 year.

Vegetable Oil

You'll need a good supply of oil for browning, deep-frying, stir-frying, baking and making salad dressings.

Store unopened vegetable oil at room temperature away from the light for a year or longer. Store opened bottles of oil in your refrigerator.

Oil you've used for deep-frying can be used over again. To clean oil, heat to 350F (175C). Carefully add pieces of peeled fresh potato. The color of the oil will lighten and particles will adhere to the potato. The oil will return to its original flavor. To strain out any remaining food particles left after deep-frying, pour cooled oil through a double thickness of cheesecloth. Store the oil in a covered jar in the refrigerator. As long as used oil is light and clear and does not retain a strong aroma of cooked foods, it can be used several times.

Vegetables

See Fruits & Vegetables, page 14.

Wheat

See Wheat, page 94.

Yogurt

Yogurt can be stored 2 to 3 weeks in your refrigerator. Make your own yogurt with 1 tablespoon of fresh yogurt and reconstituted powdered milk; see below.

Freeze-dried yogurt starter will keep in your freezer for as long as 2 years, in your refrigerator for 1 year and at room temperature for 6 months. Call health-food stores in your area to find out which ones carry freeze-dried starter.

For more information on using yogurt, see *Yogurt Cookery*, published by HP Books.

How to Make Yogurt

If you are using prepared yogurt as your starter, place about 1 tablespoon of the starter in a small bowl and let it stand at room temperature. If you are using freeze-dried starter, place it in a small bowl.

Pour 1 quart of milk into a medium saucepan. You can use reconstituted instant milk powder, fresh whole milk or a mixture of the two. A little canned milk or cream will add body and richness to the finished yogurt. Heat the milk over medium heat until bubbles appear around the edges. Do not let it come to a full boil. Remove the saucepan from the heat and let the milk cool to about 110F (45C) on a candy thermometer. Ladle about 1/3 cup of the warm milk into the bowl containing the yogurt starter. Mix it well, then stir the starter mixture into the saucepan of warm milk.

Yogurt can be incubated in a yogurt maker. They are inexpensive and very efficient. Yogurt can also be incubated in a covered bowl on top of your refrigerator wrapped in a heavy towel or thermal blanket. This is not a no-fail method. If you don't have a yogurt maker, place an oven thermometer in your oven. Preheat the oven to 150F (65C) or 200F (95C) and leave the oven door open until the thermometer registers 120F (50C). Pour the yogurt mixture into a warmed bowl. Cover it and place it in the oven. Close the oven door and turn off the heat. Do not open the oven door for several hours. If yogurt incubates overnight, you will not be tempted to open the oven door and the yogurt will be ready in the morning.

Carlene Richardson Tejada & Carroll Porter Latham

Carlene Richardson Tejada studied English Literature in her home state of New Hampshire, then moved to New York to get her master's degree. She has traveled extensively, including a year spent teaching English in El Salvador with her husband. Her experiences abroad have given Carlene a great love of international cooking. This enthusiasm is evident in the exotic recipes included in this book.

Carroll Porter Latham has a master's degree in home economics and has taught with the Cooperative Extension Services in Wyoming, Utah and Arizona. She is a member of the Mormon Church. The Church encourages its members to store a year's supply of household necessities as a safeguard against future uncer-

tainties. Working as a home economist, Carroll has seen the practice of storing food come to the rescue in times of financial need and natural disaster.

As working mothers, Carlene and Carroll know the difficulties of combining a career with looking after a family. One area where they have become expert in saving time and money is the weekly shopping. They have managed to reduce the time spent on this chore by keeping well stocked cupboards and freezers.

Carlene and Carroll have been colleagues for several years. They recently decided to share the many storage-based recipes that have evolved from their busy lives and collaborate on this book.

Time Schedule For Storage

Temperature and light are 2 factors you must control in storage areas. Pantry temperature should be 45F to 70F (5C to 20C). Refrigerator temperature should be 35F to 45F (0C to 5C). Freezer temperature should be 0F (−20C). Be sure your storage areas are dark.

Foods to Store	Quantity Per Person For 6 Months	Length of Storage Time	Special Instructions
Beans, Dried Legumes	7 lbs.	5 to 10 years	Store in pantry in airtight metal or rigid plastic containers. Keep dry.
Bread	10 lbs.	6 months	Store in freezer. Double-bag loaves to keep out moisture.
Buttermilk Powder	Optional	1 to 2 years	Store in pantry. Keep cool and dry. Refrigerate after opening.
Butter or Margarine	7 lbs.	6 to 9 months	Store in freezer.

Cereals
   Non-Instant
   Instant or Cold
	20 lbs.	
		6 to 12 months
		2 to 6 months
			Store in pantry in airtight metal or rigid plastic containers.

Eggs
   Fresh
   Water Glass
   Dried
	180 Servings	
		4 to 5 weeks
		3 to 6 months
		1 to 3 years
			
			Refrigerate.
			Store in refrigerator or pantry.
			Store in pantry. Keep cool and dry.

Flour
   All-Purpose
   Whole-Wheat
	20 lbs.	
		12 to 18 months
		6 months
			Store in pantry in airtight metal or rigid plastic containers. Keep cool and dry.

Fruits
   Canned
   Frozen
    Citrus
   Dried or
    Dehydrated
	185 Servings	
		2 to 5 years
		9 to 12 months
		2 to 3 months
		10 to 20 years
			Amounts will vary according to family preference. Include some citrus. Store home canned fruits in dark areas.

Honey	10 lbs.	Indefinite	Store in pantry in glass or rigid plastic containers.

Meats, Fish, Poultry
   Canned
   Frozen
   Dried or
    Dehydrated
	52 servings	
		1 to 3 years
		4 to 9 months
		10 to 15 years
			Store in pantry or freezer.

Foods to Store	Quantity Per Person For 6 Months	Length of Storage Time	Special Instructions

Milk
  Powdered
 	
  Evaporated
	185 qts.	
		1 to 2 years
		
		1 to 2 years
			Store in pantry in airtight metal or rigid plastic containers. Keep cool and dry. See page 15.

Pasta	20 lbs.	9 to 12 months	Store in pantry in airtight metal or rigid plastic containers. Keep dry.

Peanut Butter
  Emulsified
  Old-fashioned
    (separates)
	5 lbs.	
		1 year
		3 months
			Store in pantry. Keep cool to prevent rancidity.

Rice
  White
  Brown
	20 lbs.	
		3 to 5 years
		6 to 8 months
			Store in pantry in airtight metal or rigid plastic containers. Keep cool and dry.

Sugar
  White
  Brown
	50 lbs.	
		Indefinite
		Indefinite
			Store in pantry in airtight metal or rigid plastic containers. Keep dry.

Salt	2-1/2 lbs.	Indefinite	Store in pantry in airtight metal or rigid plastic containers. Keep dry.
Vegetable Shortening	8 lbs.	9 to 12 months	Store in pantry.
Vegetable Oil	3 to 5 qts.	9 to 12 months	Amount will vary with baking done. Animal fat content shortens time. Refrigerate opened bottles of oil.
TVP (Textured Vegetable Protein)	Optional	1 to 2 years	Store in pantry in airtight metal or rigid plastic containers. Keep cool and dry.

Vegetables
  Canned
  Frozen
  Dried or
    Dehydrated
  Root Vegetables
	185 Servings	
		2 to 5 years
		9 to 12 months
		10 to 20 years
		
		1 to 9 months
			Include green, white and yellow vegetables. Store in pantry or freezer.
			
			See pages 4 and 14.

Water	7 gallons per week	3 to 12 months	Store in pantry in glass or plastic. See page 7.
Wheat	75 lbs.	Indefinite	Treat wheat before storing. See page 94.

Your first meal of the day may be a light breakfast, a hearty brunch or just a quick bite of fruit. Whatever way you choose to break your fast, stocking up for breakfasts is a good way to begin living with stored foods.

A good stock of breakfast supplies in your cupboard, will help you maintain a balanced diet. This means no more early morning trips to the store, fewer unbudgeted grocery expenses, and convenience as close as your storage cupboard.

You may prefer other basic foods. The advantage of basic breakfast supplies is that most of

Breakfasts

them need no special storage considerations. Opened bottles of vegetable oil, opened jars of jams, jellies and peanut butter are best stored in your refrigerator. Butter or margarine can be refrigerated or frozen. Eggs can be frozen. Many other foods can be kept at room temperature for weeks or months at a time. See the table on pages 20 and 21 for storage times of individual foods.

If you can't get along without fresh whole eggs, they are not beyond the realm of possibility. For storing fresh whole eggs in water glass, or *sodium silicate*, see page 13.

If you have a freezer, put in a supply of bacon, link sausages and ground pork to make Breakfast Sausage. Add several kinds of hard cheese and cans of frozen juices. Instructions for freezing eggs are on pages 12 and 13. Packages of frozen fruit and frozen potatoes will come in handy. Buy or make bread and stack it in your freezer.

Canned hash, canned beans and canned ham will be useful. If you're planning some festive breakfasts or brunches, store some cans of tomatoes, mixed vegetables and green chilies. You'll use them in our recipes for Poached Eggs Mexican-Style and Early Bird Quiche.

Whole-wheat kernels, also called *berries*, raisins, wheat germ, honey, nuts and sunflower seeds add appetizing flavor and texture as well as nutrition to your breakfasts. Store whole-wheat kernels in a cool, dry place.

If coffee, cocoa and tea or herb tea are breakfast drinks in your house, buy enough to last several weeks. Stock up on sugar, honey, powdered milk or cream, dried mint or cloves—whatever you use with your breakfast beverage.

Unsweetened cocoa powder is an excellent flavoring for baking as well as a popular beverage ingredient. Keep at least 2 large containers on hand.

Dried yogurt starter is not a basic necessity but the nutritional value and versatility of yogurt qualifies it as a staple food. Include a few packets of dried yogurt starter in your basic supplies. Instructions for making your own yogurt are on page 18. You'll discover Apple-Yogurt Sunrise is a refreshing, energy-packed way to start your day. The recipe is in this section.

Birthday Breakfast

Melon Balls
Mom's Waffled French Toast, page 24
Honey Butter, page 25
Dutch Honey, page 27
Chocolate Chug-a-Lug, page 26
Breakfast Cookies, page 27

Creamy Oatmeal

Start a cold winter day with a hot nourishing breakfast.

3 cups water
1-2/3 cups rolled oats
1/4 teaspoon salt
2 tablespoons brown sugar

2 tablespoons wheat germ
1/4 cup raisins
About 1-1/2 cups milk

Combine water, oats, salt, brown sugar, wheat germ and raisins in a medium saucepan. Bring to a boil; reduce heat. Simmer uncovered 5 minutes, stirring occasionally. Cover and remove from heat. Let stand 2 to 3 minutes. Serve in cereal bowls with milk. Makes 4 servings.

Easy Granola

Rolled whole-wheat has a nut-like flavor.

3/4 cup honey
1/3 cup butter or margarine
4 cups rolled oats or rolled whole-wheat
1-1/2 cups shredded coconut

1 cup coarsely chopped walnuts or pecans
3/4 cup pine nuts or sunflower seeds
1 tablespoon ground cinnamon
3/4 teaspoon salt

Place honey and butter or margarine in a small heavy saucepan over low heat. Stir occasionally until butter or margarine is melted. Preheat oven to 350F (175C). Combine remaining ingredients in a 13" x 9" baking pan. Pour honey mixture over rolled oats or rolled whole-wheat mixture, stirring to distribute evenly. Bake 30 minutes or until golden brown. Cool in baking pan on a rack, stirring occasionally. Store in an airtight container at room temperature. Makes about 6-1/2 cups.

Apple-Yogurt Sunrise

No cooking required for this nourishing treat.

4 cups Homemade Yogurt, page 18, or
   plain yogurt
1/4 cup apple butter

4 to 6 teaspoons honey
1/2 teaspoon ground cinnamon

Stir yogurt in a small bowl until creamy. Combine remaining ingredients in another small bowl or cup; mix well. Stir apple butter mixture into yogurt. Refrigerate until ready to serve. Spoon into 4 bowls. Makes 4 servings.

Mom's Waffled French Toast

Dutch Honey, page 27, and orange slices make this a glorious brunch dish.

1/3 cup finely chopped walnuts or pecans
1/4 cup sugar
1/2 teaspoon ground cinnamon
2 eggs, beaten, or equivalent
1/4 teaspoon salt

1/2 cup milk
10 slices day-old white or
   whole-wheat bread
About 1/2 cup butter or margarine,
   room temperature

Preheat a waffle iron according to manufacturer's instructions. Combine nuts, sugar and cinnamon in a small bowl; set aside. Place eggs in a shallow 1-quart dish; beat in salt and milk. Generously spread both sides of bread with butter or margarine. Dip bread into egg mixture to coat both sides. Place 1 slice of bread on preheated waffle iron. Sprinkle about 2 teaspoons nut mixture on bread. Close waffle iron. Bake until bread is golden brown. Remove from waffle iron. Repeat dipping and baking with remaining bread slices. Makes 4 servings.

How to Make Mom's Waffled French Toast

1/If you are using dried whole eggs, mix them with liquid. Follow package directions for the amount of liquid.

2/Dip buttered bread into egg mixture to coat both sides. Sprinkle nut mixture on egg-coated bread.

Honey Butter *Photo on page 125.*

There's no better treat than this spread on fresh-baked bread.

1/2 cup butter or margarine,
   room temperature
1 egg yolk or equivalent

1/4 teaspoon vanilla extract
1/2 cup honey

Beat butter or margarine in a small bowl until creamy and airy, about 1 minute. Use an electric beater for a lighter and more airy mixture. Beat in egg yolk and vanilla. Gradually beat in honey. Cover and store in refrigerator. Serve at room temperature. Makes about 1 cup.

Freezer Red Raspberry Jam *Photo on cover, page 52 and page 102.*

Enjoy homemade jam on rolls, pancakes or waffles.

3 (10-oz.) pkgs. frozen red raspberries,
   thawed
5 cups sugar

1 pkg. powdered pectin
3/4 cup water

Place a fine sieve over a large bowl. Press raspberries through sieve with the back of a spoon. Discard seeds. Stir sugar into raspberry pulp. Let stand about 20 minutes, stirring occasionally. In a medium saucepan, combine powdered pectin and water. Bring to a boil over medium heat. Boil 1 minute, stirring constantly. Stir in raspberry mixture. Cook and stir over medium heat about 2 minutes. Pour into 8 or 9 sterile 8-ounce jelly glasses or jars. Top with sterile lids. Arrange on a rack to cool. Let stand at room temperature at least 24 hours. Store in freezer 6 months or in refrigerator 6 to 8 weeks. Makes about 8 cups.

English Lemon Curd *Photo on page 102.*

Spread this on toast, muffins or waffles.

4 eggs, beaten, or equivalent
3/4 cup sugar
1/4 cup lemon juice

1/4 cup butter or margarine,
   room temperature
Pinch of salt

Combine all ingredients in the top of a double boiler. Stir to blend. Cook over simmering water 20 to 30 minutes, stirring occasionally. When mixture has thickened, remove from heat. If mixture contains any lumps, stir briskly. Cool to room temperature. Cover and refrigerate or freeze. Makes about 2 cups.

Breakfast Sausage

Make your own spicy sausage patties.

1 lb. ground pork or beef
2 tablespoons to 1/4 cup vinegar
1/2 teaspoon ground coriander
1 teaspoon ground rubbed sage
1/2 teaspoon salt

1/8 teaspoon ground allspice
1/2 teaspoon dry mustard
1/4 teaspoon garlic powder
1/4 teaspoon pepper

Combine all ingredients in a medium bowl, adjusting the amount of vinegar to your taste. Mix well. Cover and refrigerate at least overnight to blend flavors. Sausage will keep 1 week in refrigerator. Preheat a medium skillet over medium heat. With your hands, shape sausage into 4 thin patties. Cook on both sides in preheated skillet over medium heat until each side is crisp and browned. Makes four 1/4-pound patties.

Chocolate Chug-a-Lug

Cold, sweet and light—perfect for a summer brunch.

1 egg or equivalent
1 cup milk
1/4 cup sugar
2 tablespoons unsweetened cocoa powder

2 tablespoons lemon juice
1/2 slice white or whole-wheat bread
4 ice cubes

Combine all ingredients in a blender. Process 15 to 20 seconds until ice cubes are finely broken and mixture is frothy. Makes 2 servings.

Mixes

Ingredients for making your own mixes are easier to store than the mixes themselves. Basic Baking Mix is on page 121, and Treasure House Beef Mix—a frozen ground beef mixture—is on page 88. For additional information and recipes for making mixes, see *Make-A-Mix Cookery* and *More Make-A-Mix Cookery*, published by HPBooks.

Breakfast Cookies

These scrumptious cookies will disappear in a hurry.

1 cup bite-size shredded wheat
1 teaspoon grated orange peel
1/4 cup chopped walnuts or pecans
1/4 cup hulled sunflower seeds
1 cup flake cereal such as cornflakes or
  bran flakes

1/4 cup sugar
2 eggs, beaten, or equivalent
1/2 cup raisins
1/2 teaspoon vanilla extract
1/4 to 1/3 cup graham cracker crumbs
  (about 3 square crackers)

Crumble shredded wheat in a plastic bag. Place crumbled shredded wheat in a medium bowl. Mix in orange peel, walnuts or pecans, sunflower seeds and flake cereal. Combine sugar, eggs and raisins in a medium saucepan. Stir over medium heat until mixture thickens, 3 to 5 minutes; do not scorch. Remove from heat and stir in vanilla. Add shredded wheat mixture; mix well. Cool slightly. With lightly floured hands, roll 1 rounded teaspoon of mixture into a ball. Roll in graham cracker crumbs. Place on a platter or baking sheet. Repeat with remaining mixture. Cover cookies and refrigerate. Makes about 20 cookies.

Dutch Honey

Perfect for pancakes, waffles or ice cream.

1 cup dark corn syrup
1 cup sugar

1 cup evaporated milk

Combine corn syrup and sugar in a medium saucepan. Bring to a simmer over medium heat, stirring occasionally. Simmer until sugar is dissolved, about 4 minutes. Remove from heat. Cool in saucepan on a rack about 3 minutes. Slowly stir in evaporated milk. Pour into a storage container. Cover and store in refrigerator. Serve warm or cold from a syrup pitcher. Makes about 2-1/2 cups.

Cocoa Izalco   Photo on page 29.

Spiced cocoa is a popular breakfast beverage throughout Latin America.

3 cups milk
1/4 cup unsweetened cocoa powder
1/4 to 1/3 cup sugar
1/2 teaspoon ground cinnamon

1/4 cup hot water
1/4 teaspoon almond extract
8 cinnamon sticks, if desired
Non-dairy whipped topping, if desired

Heat milk in a medium saucepan over medium heat. Combine cocoa powder, sugar and cinnamon in a small bowl. Add hot water. Mix thoroughly to remove all lumps. Stir in almond extract. Whisk cocoa mixture into hot milk. Pour into 4 mugs. If desired, add 2 cinnamon sticks and a dollop of whipped topping to each mug. Serve immediately. Makes 4 servings.

Poached Eggs Mexican-Style

For a marvelous brunch, serve these eggs with Refried Beans, page 68, and warm tortillas.

4 frozen or fresh whole eggs
1 tablespoon vegetable oil
1 small onion, chopped
1 (4-oz.) can diced green chilies
1 (16-oz.) can tomatoes, drained, chopped
1/4 teaspoon garlic powder
1/4 teaspoon pepper

1/4 teaspoon dried leaf oregano, crushed
1/4 teaspoon salt
2/3 cup shredded Monterey Jack cheese
  (about 3-1/2 oz.)
1 orange, thinly sliced for garnish
1 lime, thinly sliced for garnish

If using frozen eggs, remove from freezer about 1 hour before serving. Place each frozen egg in a cup or small bowl. Let stand at room temperature to thaw partially. About 20 minutes before serving, preheat a large skillet over medium heat. Add oil. Cook onion in oil until tender but not browned. Add chilies, tomatoes, garlic powder, pepper, oregano and salt. Cook over medium-low heat until some moisture has evaporated and mixture is blended, 5 to 10 minutes. Stir occasionally. Sprinkle 1/3 cup cheese evenly over tomato mixture. Cover and cook until cheese begins to melt, 2 to 3 minutes. Place eggs on top of melting cheese. Sprinkle 1/3 cup cheese over eggs. Cover and cook until eggs are set and cheese is melted, 5 to 10 minutes. To serve, slip a spatula under tomato mixture and 1 egg. Lift onto a plate. When all eggs are served, spoon remaining tomato mixture over each serving. Garnish with orange and lime slices. Makes 4 servings.

Crunchy Stacks

Your reputation as a breakfast cook will soar!

3 eggs, beaten, or equivalent
1/2 cup milk
1/3 cup crushed cornflakes
2 tablespoons butter, margarine or
  bacon drippings

8 slices white bread
3 tablespoons peanut butter
3 tablespoons jam
Powdered sugar

Mix eggs and milk in a shallow bowl. Spread crushed cornflakes on a plate or small baking sheet. Preheat a large skillet. Melt about 1/2 tablespoon butter, margarine or bacon drippings in skillet. Dip bread in egg mixture to coat both sides. Cook 2 pieces of egg-coated bread until browned on 1 side only. Remove from skillet; place uncooked-side down in crushed cornflakes. Spread 1 slice on cooked side with about 2 teaspoons peanut butter. Spread other slice with about 2 teaspoons jam. Press jam-side down on bread with peanut butter to make a sandwich. If necessary, press cornflakes into bread. Return sandwiches to skillet and cook until uncooked sides are browned. Sprinkle with powdered sugar. Serve immediately. Repeat to make 3 more sandwiches, adding more butter, margarine or bacon drippings to skillet as needed. Makes 4 servings.

Poached Eggs Mexican-Style; Refried Beans, page 68; and Cocoa Izalco, page 27

Early Bird Quiche

Serve this marvelously light quiche this weekend.

Flaky Pie Pastry for single-crust pie,
  page 113
1 (16-oz.) can mixed vegetables
5 eggs, separated, or equivalent
About 1/2 cup evaporated milk
3 tablespoons imitation bacon bits

1 tablespoon dried minced onion
3/4 teaspoon salt
Pinch of pepper, if desired
1-1/2 cups shredded mild Cheddar cheese
  (6 oz.)

Prepare Flaky Pie Pastry. Roll out dough and line a 9-inch pie pan following directions on page 113. Do not prick crust. Heat oven to 400F (205C). Drain vegetables, reserving liquid; set aside. If using dried egg yolks and dried egg whites, rehydrate separately. Beat egg yolks in a medium bowl until pale and thickened. Pour reserved liquid from mixed vegetables into a 2-cup measure. Add enough evaporated milk to vegetable liquid to make 1-1/2 cups. Stir into beaten eggs with bacon bits, onion, salt and pepper, if desired. Beat egg whites until stiff peaks form. Fold beaten egg whites into egg yolk mixture. Sprinkle cheese over bottom of crust. Top with drained vegetables. Spoon egg mixture over vegetables and spread evenly. Bake 10 minutes. Reduce heat to 375F (190C). Continue baking 40 to 50 minutes until egg mixture is firm and crust is golden. Remove from oven and cool 5 minutes on a rack. Makes 6 servings.

Peaches & Hash

A festive dish for weekend guests.

1/2 cup beef or vegetable broth
1/2 cup tomato sauce
2 tablespoons dried minced onion
2 tablespoons mixed dried chopped peppers
1-1/2 teaspoons Worcestershire sauce
Salt and pepper to taste

1 (12-oz.) can roast beef, shredded
1 (16-oz.) can potatoes, diced
1-1/2 teaspoons vegetable oil or
  bacon drippings
1 (1-lb., 13-oz.) can peach halves, drained
2 teaspoons brown sugar

Combine broth and tomato sauce in a medium bowl. Stir in onion, peppers, Worcestershire sauce and salt and pepper. Stir in beef and potatoes. Let stand 10 to 15 minutes to rehydrate onion and peppers. Preheat a medium skillet over medium heat. Add oil or bacon drippings. Cook meat mixture, stirring occasionally, until blended and most of the liquid has evaporated, 15 to 20 minutes. Mound cooked hash on a broiler-proof platter or in a small baking pan. Surround hash with peach halves placed cut-side up. Spoon 1/4 teaspoon brown sugar in center of each peach half. Broil until peaches are hot and brown sugar is melted, about 2 minutes. Serve immediately. Makes 4 or 5 servings.

Variation

Peaches & Vegetable Hash: Stir 1/4 cup diced cooked carrot or turnip into meat mixture before cooking.

How to Make Early Bird Quiche

1/If you are using dried egg whites, beat them with water until stiff. Follow package directions for the amount of water.

2/Sprinkle cheese over bottom of crust. Top with drained vegetables. Fold beaten egg whites into egg yolk mixture.

Busy Morning Pancakes & Waffles

The lightest, most tender pancakes and waffles you can imagine!

1 teaspoon sugar
2 cups Basic Baking Mix, page 121

1 egg, beaten, or equivalent
1 cup water or milk

Preheat griddle or preheat waffle iron according to manufacturer's instructions. In a medium bowl, stir sugar into Basic Baking Mix. Stir egg into water or milk, then stir into sugar and Basic Baking Mix until moistened. Batter will be lumpy. When a drop of water skips over the griddle surface, the griddle is hot enough. Bake pancakes on hot griddle until edges become dry, then turn with a spatula and bake other side. Bake waffles according to manufacturer's instructions. Makes about ten 3-inch pancakes or 4 large waffles.

Variation
Cornmeal Pancakes & Waffles: Substitute 1/2 cup cornmeal for 1/2 cup Basic Baking Mix.

If you've ever been caught raiding the refrigerator between meals, you'll appreciate this group of recipes.

When you want something light but tasty and quick to fix, try Plowman's Snack. Keep a loaf of party rye in your freezer and a container of Mixed Fruit Chutney in your refrigerator beside a jar of cheese spread. Then you'll always have the makings for this savory treat.

Chicken-Bacon Sandwich Spread, Pineapple-Ham Sandwich Spread and Tuna Sandwich Spread are delectable as sandwich fillings or top-

Appetizers & Snacks

pings for crackers. They are a successful trio in New Year's Sandwich Loaf.

One popular snack food is popcorn. Buy unpopped popcorn in large bags and pour it into containers with tight-fitting lids. If popcorn has been stored for a long time and is a bit dry, sprinkle a few drops of water into the storage container and cover it tightly. Shake the container well before putting it back on the shelf. The next time you make popcorn, it will be more tender.

Popcorn can be a snack, an appetizer or even a dessert. For an appetizer, try Herbed Popcorn. For a mid-afternoon or late-night snack, Parmesan Herbed Popcorn will satisfy most cravings. Experiment with other seasonings. Once you've

poured melted butter or margarine over popcorn, you can sprinkle it with any flavoring you want. A mixture of cinnamon and sugar on buttered popcorn is an appealing mid-morning snack or a different dessert. Flavored salts, such as garlic or celery are a welcome change.

Tantalizing Trail Mix is a delicious and nutritious make-ahead snack. Mix up a large batch and divide it into smaller portions for after-school snacks, energy boosters or a quick breakfast on the run. Fill small plastic bags with about 1/2 cup of Tantalizing Trail Mix. Close each bag with a twist tie and pack the filled bags into a large container that has a tight-fitting lid. With these stored in a cool dry place, you're ready to hand out instant pick-me-ups when needed.

Giving a dinner party? Mushroom Soufflé, Liver Pâté, or Greek Bean Salad will bring the right touch of sophistication to an important evening. Liver Pâté can be made weeks ahead and stored in your freezer until the special occasion.

Lunch on the Trail

Tantalizing Trail Mix, below
Plowman's Snack, page 36
Chicken-Bacon Sandwiches, page 38
Orange-Carrot Cookies, page 155
Apple Juice

Tantalizing Trail Mix

For a crowd of hikers, add another cup of raisins and plenty of nuts.

1 (6-oz.) pkg. diced mixed dried fruit
1/2 cup raisins
1/2 cup hulled sunflower seeds

3/4 cup cocktail peanuts or cashews
3/4 cup carob pieces or chocolate pieces

Mix all ingredients in a canister with a tight-fitting lid or in a plastic bag. Secure bag with a twist tie. Makes about 4 cups.

Mushroom Soufflé

A delicious combination of flavors.

1 to 2 tablespoons dry breadcrumbs
1 (4-oz.) can mushroom stems and
  pieces, undrained
1/3 cup instant milk powder
About 3/4 cup water
3 tablespoons butter or margarine
3 tablespoons all-purpose flour

3 eggs, beaten, or equivalent
1/4 teaspoon salt
Pepper to taste
1/8 teaspoon garlic powder
1/8 teaspoon poultry seasoning
1/8 teaspoon dried leaf basil, crushed
3 egg whites or equivalent

Butter a 1-1/2-quart soufflé dish or casserole and sprinkle with breadcrumbs. Preheat oven to 375F (190C). Drain mushrooms, reserving liquid. Stir milk powder into mushroom liquid. Add water to measure 1 cup. Stir to blend. Finely chop mushrooms; set aside. In a medium saucepan, melt butter or margarine over medium heat. Thoroughly blend in flour. In a small saucepan, bring milk mixture almost to a boil. Pour into flour mixture, stirring constantly. Cook and stir until sauce is smooth and thickened. Set aside to cool. Beat eggs into cooled sauce. Stir in chopped mushrooms, salt, pepper, garlic powder, poultry seasoning and basil. Beat egg whites until stiff but not dry. Slowly pour egg mixture over beaten egg whites. Gently fold in. Pour into prepared dish. Bake 30 to 40 minutes until a knife inserted off center comes out clean. Serve immediately. Makes 4 to 6 servings.

Sweet & Sour Chicken Wings

Serve with Parslied Rice, page 73, for a main dish.

18 chicken wings
1 tablespoon dried chopped celery
1 teaspoon salt
1/4 teaspoon pepper
2 cups water
3 tablespoons cornstarch
1/2 cup packed brown sugar
1/2 cup white vinegar

1/3 cup soy sauce
1/3 cup chili sauce or ketchup
2 tablespoons butter or margarine
3 medium carrots, cut in
  thin rounds
1 cup green pepper strips
1 (16-oz.) can pineapple chunks,
  drained, cut in half

Wash and drain chicken wings. Remove and discard tips of wings. In a large saucepan or Dutch oven, combine wings, celery, salt, pepper and water. Bring to a boil; reduce heat. Cover and simmer over medium heat 30 minutes. In a small bowl, mix cornstarch, brown sugar and vinegar until sugar has dissolved. Stir in soy sauce and chili sauce or ketchup. Remove wings from broth. Set wings aside and keep warm. Strain broth; return to saucepan or Dutch oven. Stir in cornstarch mixture. Stir over medium heat until sauce is clear and thickened; set aside. In a large skillet, melt butter or margarine. Stir in carrot rounds. Cover and cook over low heat about 2 minutes. Stir in cooked chicken wings, green pepper strips and pineapple. Cook about 2 minutes. Turn into a large chafing dish. Pour sweet and sour sauce over chicken wing mixture. Makes 18 appetizer servings.

Liver Pâté

Serve on toasted homemade bread or rye crackers.

2 tablespoons dried minced onion
2 tablespoons water
2 tablespoons butter or margarine
1 lb. chicken livers
1 (4-oz.) can mushroom stems and
  pieces, drained
1/2 teaspoon garlic powder
1/4 teaspoon ground marjoram

1/2 teaspoon dried leaf basil
1/4 teaspoon salt
1/4 teaspoon pepper
About 2 tablespoons evaporated milk
About 2 tablespoons sherry, if desired
Freeze-dried chives
2 tablespoons butter or margarine, melted

Combine onion and water in a small bowl. Let stand 10 to 15 minutes to rehydrate onion. Melt 2 tablespoons butter or margarine in a large skillet over medium heat. Add chicken livers. Brown lightly, turning frequently, 5 to 10 minutes. Add mushrooms, rehydrated onion, garlic powder, marjoram and basil. Cook 5 to 10 minutes longer, stirring frequently. Cut through 1 chicken liver. If still very pink, cook a little longer. Remove skillet from heat; cool slightly. Stir in salt, pepper and evaporated milk. Add sherry, if desired. Let stand until completely cooled. Put a fourth of the cooled mixture into a blender or food processor. Process until smooth, adding 1 teaspoon evaporated milk or sherry if necessary for easier processing. Spoon into a ramekin or small serving bowl. Sprinkle with chives. Repeat with remaining chicken liver mixture, processing a fourth of the mixture at a time and spooning each fourth into a separate ramekin. Spoon 2 tablespoons melted butter or margarine equally over pâté. Cover and chill. Store in refrigerator up to 2 weeks. Store in freezer up to 1 month. Makes about 1-1/2 cups.

Freezer Storage

Some refrigerator-freezers are not designed for long-term storage. Keep a cold-temperature thermometer in your refrigerator-freezer and periodically check the temperature. It should be at 0F (−20C) or colder. Free-standing freezers operate most efficiently when kept completely full.

Package home-frozen foods in small quantities. The centers of large packages are slow to freeze and cause the freezer to run longer than necessary. Arrange containers throughout the freezer until they are frozen solid.

How to Make Liver Pâté

1/Put cooled liver mixture into a blender or food processor a fourth at a time. Process until smooth.

2/Spoon melted butter or margarine over pâté in ramekins.

Greek Bean Salad

If you have fresh spinach, use it to line the salad plates.

1 cup dried Great Northern beans
4 cups water
1 tablespoon vegetable oil
1 bay leaf
2 tablespoons vegetable oil
2 tablespoons olive oil
1 small onion, chopped
1/4 cup tomato juice

1/4 teaspoon garlic powder
1/8 teaspoon ground thyme
1 tablespoon dried leaf parsley
2 tablespoons lime juice or lemon juice
1/2 teaspoon salt
1/8 teaspoon pepper
Ripe olives

Sort and rinse beans. Bring water to a boil in a medium saucepan. Add 1 tablespoon vegetable oil and bay leaf. Drop in beans a few at a time, maintaining a rolling boil. Cover and reduce heat. Cook until tender, about 1-1/2 hours. Drain beans, reserving liquid for another use. Remove bay leaf. Heat 2 tablespoons vegetable oil and olive oil in a small skillet. Sauté onion in skillet over medium-low heat. When onion is tender, remove skillet from heat. Stir in tomato juice, garlic powder, thyme and parsley. Pour over cooked beans. Sprinkle with lime or lemon juice, salt and pepper. Serve on individual salad plates. Garnish each serving with 1 or 2 ripe olives. Makes 4 servings.

Herbed Popcorn

So irresistible you'll want to make 2 batches!

3 tablespoons butter or margarine
1 teaspoon Herb Seasoning, page 54
2 tablespoons vegetable oil

1/2 cup popcorn
1/4 teaspoon salt

Melt butter or margarine over low heat. Stir in Herb Seasoning. Let stand while making popcorn. Combine oil and popcorn in a popcorn popper or a covered, large heavy pot. Heat over medium-high heat until 1 kernel pops. Shake popper or pot over heat until popping stops. Pour popcorn into a large bowl. Drizzle with butter mixture and sprinkle with salt. Mix well. Makes 10 to 12 cups.

Variation

Cheese Herbed Popcorn: Sprinkle popcorn with 2 tablespoons grated Parmesan cheese before adding salt.

Plowman's Snack

Every London pub has its own version of this traditional combination.

1/2 cup pasteurized process cheese spread
About 8 slices party rye bread

1/2 cup Mixed Fruit Chutney, page 145,
   or other chutney

Spread 1 tablespoon cheese on a slice of bread. Top with 1 tablespoon chutney. Repeat with remaining cheese, bread and chutney. Makes about 8 appetizers.

Fruit Balls

A great way to get more milk into children's diets.

6 tablespoons unsweetened frozen orange
   juice concentrate, partially thawed
1/2 teaspoon lemon juice
2 cups powdered sugar
1/4 cup butter or margarine,
   room temperature

1/2 cup flaked coconut
About 1 cup instant or non-instant
   milk powder
About 1/2 cup cornflake crumbs

In a large bowl, combine orange juice concentrate, lemon juice and powdered sugar. Beat in butter or margarine and coconut. Stir in enough milk powder to make mixture stiff enough to shape into 3/4-inch balls. Roll balls in cornflake crumbs. Refrigerate or freeze until served. Will keep in refrigerator 1 to 2 weeks, in freezer 3 to 6 months. Makes about 40 Fruit Balls.

Plowman's Snack and Mixed Fruit Chutney, page 145

Pineapple-Ham Sandwich Spread

Delicious on rye bread or wheat crackers.

**1/2 (8-oz.) can crushed pineapple in
  unsweetened juice**
1 (6-3/4-oz.) can chunked and ground ham

4 whole water chestnuts
About 3 tablespoons mayonnaise
Pinch of ground cloves, more if desired

Place pineapple in a strainer. Drain well, pressing with a spoon to extract all liquid. Mince ham and water chestnuts with a sharp knife. Combine drained pineapple, minced ham and water chestnuts, mayonnaise and cloves in a small bowl. Mix well. Refrigerate until ready to use. Add more mayonnaise and cloves, if desired. Makes enough sandwich spread for 2 or 3 sandwiches.

Chicken-Bacon Sandwich Spread

A different combination for your lunch sandwiches.

1/4 lb. bacon, diced, cooked, drained
**1 (6-1/4-oz.) can chunked and ground
  chicken, drained, chopped**
3 tablespoons mayonnaise

1/8 teaspoon garlic powder
1/8 teaspoon celery salt
Pinch of pepper

Mix all ingredients in a medium bowl. Refrigerate until ready to serve. Makes enough sandwich spread for 2 or 3 sandwiches.

Tuna Sandwich Spread

Use sandwich spreads in New Year's Sandwich Loaf, page 137.

1 (6-1/2-oz.) can tuna, drained, flaked
3 tablespoons chopped fresh onion
Pinch of pepper

2 tablespoons sweet relish
3 tablespoons mayonnaise

Mix all ingredients in a medium bowl. Refrigerate until ready to serve. Makes enough sandwich spread for 2 or 3 sandwiches.

Many good cooks' reputations have been made with a pot of hot flavorful soup. Serve freshly baked bread with a bowl of steaming homemade soup and you're well on your way to the Cookery Hall of Fame! Bread recipes begin on page 119.

With the exception of frozen fish, frozen broth and butter or margarine, all of the basic ingredients for this section can be stored at room temperature. Packages of frozen fish are small and compact enough to fit several in a small freezer. Butter or margarine can be refrigerated or frozen. Butter-flavor granules are a good substitute for butter or margarine in soups and can be stored at room temperature. When a recipe calls for sautéing vegetables for soup in butter or margarine, you can use oil. For added flavor, stir butter-flavor granules into the soup a few minutes before serving. In most recipes, canned vegetables can be substituted for frozen vegetables.

A flavorful stock or broth is the basis of a good soup. Make your own broth as you need it or make it ahead and freeze it. Freezers are indispensable for storing homemade broth. With a supply of beef or chicken broth in your freezer, assorted vegetables and a few herbs and spices, you can make soup 2 or 3 times a week for several months! Canned broth is convenient if you have the space to store it. You can also use bouillon cubes or granules or the cooking liquid from vegetables. Add leftover beef gravy to bouillon or vegetable broth to give it extra body and flavor.

It's also a good idea to keep croutons in the freezer when you expect to store them for a long time.

The most valuable soup ingredient of all is water. In case of emergencies or water shortages, be sure to have a good supply of bottled water on hand. See page 7 for information on storing water.

Juice drained from canned vegetables such as beets and tomatoes adds wonderful flavor to soups. When you drain canned tomatoes, save the juice and refrigerate it. Within a few days use it to stretch Sierra Vista Gazpacho or make the variation for Oyster Stew. Juice from canned beets is the base for Root Cellar Soup. Add any vegetables you want or omit something you don't have on hand. For information on a root cellar, see page 4. Root vegetables can also be

fresh from your garden or bought at the supermarket. They are an economical way to add freshness to your diet.

Many cooks put fresh onions at the top of their list of absolute necessities. They often receive their inspiration for preparing a meal while chopping a fresh onion. If a lack of fresh onions inhibits your creativity, turn to page 16

and learn how you can store fresh onions for several months.

While living on stored foods, you can enjoy a variety of international foods. Be experimental and try our Black-Bean Soup. Sierra Vista Gazpacho is a delightful cold soup that originated in Spain. Be sure you have a variety of herbs and spices on hand.

Caribbean Windjammer Supper

Sliced Canned Mangoes
Black-Bean Soup, page 46
Buttermilk Corn Bread, page 128
Carroll's Salsa, page 68
Spiced Flans, page 105
Cocoa Izalco, page 27

Cream of Tomato Soup

A delicious creamy soup.

1 (28-oz.) can tomatoes	1 tablespoon sugar
1/4 teaspoon celery salt	1 teaspoon salt
3 tablespoons dried chopped onion	1/4 cup all-purpose flour
1 bay leaf	2 tablespoons butter or margarine
4 whole cloves	1 tablespoon dried leaf parsley
2 cups milk	1/4 cup croutons

Pour tomatoes with juice into a small saucepan. Place over medium-high heat. Stir in celery salt. Cut an 8-inch square of fine-mesh nylon net or three 8-inch-square layers of cheesecloth. Place onion, bay leaf and cloves on center of cloth. Pull sides of cloth together; tie with string to make a spice packet. Place spice packet in saucepan with tomatoes. Use a spoon to break up tomatoes, if necessary. Bring to a boil. Reduce heat slightly; simmer 15 minutes. Be sure spice packet is immersed in tomato juice. Stir frequently to blend flavors. Remove and discard spice packet. Press tomatoes through a sieve into a medium saucepan. Discard seeds and remaining pulp. Pour milk into another small saucepan. Place over medium heat to scald. When milk shimmers and forms bubbles around side of pan, remove from heat. Cover and keep hot. Combine sugar, salt and flour in a small bowl. Carefully but rapidly, stir flour mixture into sieved tomatoes. Continue to stir as mixture comes to a boil over medium-high heat. Reduce heat slightly. Continue to cook and stir until thickened and smooth, about 5 minutes. Stir hot milk into tomato mixture a little at a time, stirring well after each addition. Stir in butter or margarine. Reduce heat to low. Cook and stir gently 2 minutes longer. Pour soup into a soup tureen. Garnish with parsley and croutons. Makes 4 to 5 servings.

Old Pueblo Chicken Soup

Buttermilk Corn Bread, page 128, and this soup make a delightful Southwestern-style lunch.

4 cups Homemade Chicken Broth, opposite, or canned chicken broth	1/2 cup frozen whole-kernel corn
1/2 cup uncooked long-grain rice	2 canned tomatoes, chopped, drained
1/4 teaspoon ground coriander	1/4 cup lime juice
1/2 teaspoon salt	1/4 teaspoon red (cayenne) pepper
1/2 (12-1/2-oz.) can chicken, shredded, or 3/4 cup chopped cooked chicken	Salt to taste

Bring chicken broth to a boil in a large saucepan. Stir in rice, coriander and 1/2 teaspoon salt. Reduce heat to low. Cover and cook 15 minutes. Stir in chicken and corn. Cover and bring to a boil. Remove from heat. Stir in tomatoes, lime juice, red pepper and salt. Makes 4 servings.

Variation

Chinese Chicken Soup: Omit salt and lime juice. Slice 1 or 2 bean curd squares into shreds or matchsticks and stir into soup with tomatoes. Before serving, stir in 1 to 2 tablespoons soy sauce.

How to Make Cream of Tomato Soup

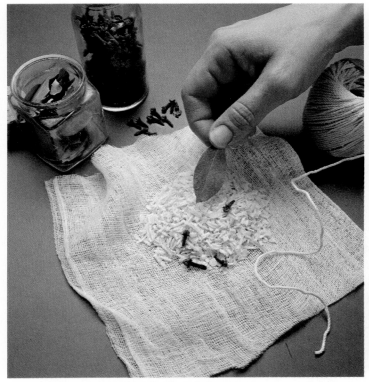

1/Place onion, bay leaf and cloves on center of cheese-cloth square. Pull sides of cloth square together and tie with string to make spice packet.

2/Stir hot milk into thickened tomato mixture a little at a time. Stir well after each addition.

Homemade Chicken Broth

Keep plenty on hand to make full-flavored soups at a moment's notice.

**1 whole chicken, cooked, meat removed,
   or equivalent in chicken bones**
2 qts. water
1 bay leaf
1 teaspoon salt
**1 medium onion, or 2 tablespoons
   dried minced onion**

1/4 cup cider vinegar
1/4 teaspoon garlic powder
1/4 teaspoon poultry seasoning
**1 tablespoon dried shredded carrots,
   if desired**
**1 tablespoon dried chopped celery,
   if desired**

Combine all ingredients in a large saucepan or pot. Bring to a boil; reduce heat. Cover and simmer 2 to 4 hours. Skim off any surface foam during cooking. Cool. Strain; discard bones and other ingredients. Pour cooled stock into storage containers. Cover and refrigerate. The fat that rises to the surface will seal the broth so it can be refrigerated 2 or 3 weeks. Stock can be frozen several months. Makes about 2 quarts of stock.

Deluxe Shrimp Bisque

Boost your culinary reputation with this richly flavored soup.

2 tablespoons hot water
2 tablespoons dried chopped green peppers
2 tablespoons dried chopped onion
1 tablespoon butter or margarine
1 (4-1/2-oz.) can shrimp, drained, rinsed,
    or 1 (6-oz.) pkg. frozen
    shelled shrimp, thawed
1 tablespoon sugar
1 teaspoon salt

1/4 teaspoon celery salt
3 tablespoons all-purpose flour
1/4 teaspoon dried leaf basil, crushed
1 bay leaf
4 whole cloves
1 (8-oz.) can tomato sauce
2-1/2 cups milk
1 cup evaporated milk

Combine hot water, green peppers and onion in a small bowl. Let stand 10 to 15 minutes to rehydrate green pepper and onion. Melt butter or margarine in a small skillet. Add rehydrated green peppers and onion. Sauté about 1 minute. Add shrimp to onion mixture. Sauté until heated through and shrimp is light pink, 4 to 7 minutes. Combine sugar, salt, celery salt, flour and basil in a small bowl. Stir until blended; set aside. Cut a 5-inch square of fine-mesh nylon net or three 5-inch-square layers of cheesecloth. Place bay leaf and cloves on center of cloth. Pull sides of cloth together; tie with string to make a spice packet. Pour tomato sauce into a medium saucepan. Add spice packet. Bring to a boil over medium-high heat. Reduce heat; simmer 15 minutes over medium-low heat to let flavors blend. Remove and discard spice packet. Slowly stir 1/2 cup whole milk into flour mixture to make a thin paste. Pour remaining whole milk and evaporated milk into a medium saucepan. Stir in flour paste. Heat and stir over medium heat until slightly thickened. Do not boil. Gradually stir hot milk mixture into hot tomato sauce. Stir in shrimp mixture. Let simmer about 2 minutes. Makes 4 to 6 servings.

Oyster Stew

A marvelous midnight supper.

1 (8-oz.) can oyster pieces, undrained
2 cups milk
2 (5.33-oz.) cans evaporated milk
    (1-1/3 cups)
1/2 teaspoon celery salt

1/4 teaspoon pepper
1 teaspoon dried leaf parsley
1 tablespoon dried minced onion
1/4 cup butter or margarine

Combine all ingredients in a medium saucepan; cover. Heat over medium-low heat without stirring. When butter or margarine has melted, stir and serve; do not boil. Makes 4 servings.

Variation

Substitute 1/2 to 1 cup juice from canned tomatoes for 1/2 to 1 cup of the milk. Add 1/4 teaspoon crushed dried leaf basil before heating.

New England Corn Chowder

Onions give this dish its special texture and flavor.

1 (15-oz.) can whole potatoes
1 (7-oz.) can whole-kernel corn,
    undrained
2 tablespoons butter or margarine
2 medium onions, cut in narrow wedges
1 (16-oz.) can cream-style corn

Water
2/3 cup instant milk powder
1 teaspoon salt
1/8 teaspoon pepper
1 tablespoon butter or margarine

Drain potatoes, reserving liquid. Cut each potato in 4 pieces. Drain whole-kernel corn, adding liquid to potato liquid. Melt 2 tablespoons butter or margarine in a large saucepan over low heat. Add onions. Sauté until tender. Add cut potatoes, cream-style corn and whole-kernel corn. Add water to reserved potato-corn liquid to measure 2 cups. Add instant milk powder. Stir until dissolved. Pour into corn-potato mixture. Stir in salt and pepper. Top chowder with 1 tablespoon butter or margarine; do not stir. Cover and heat over medium-low heat; do not boil. When butter or margarine has melted, chowder is ready to serve. Makes 4 to 6 servings.

Variation

New England Clam Chowder: Omit whole-kernel corn, cream-style corn and salt and use 1 (10-ounce) can whole baby clams. Drain clams, adding liquid to potato liquid. Rinse clams in a bowl of cold water to remove any shells. Add rinsed clams to milk mixture. Add 1 (5.33-ounce) can evaporated milk, if desired. Garnish with 1 teaspoon imitation bacon bits. Add butter or margarine; cover and heat as directed above. Makes 3 or 4 servings.

Freeze-Dried Foods

Stores specializing in food for hikers and campers usually have a wide range of freeze-dried foods. Small amounts of each food are sealed in packages containing 1 to 4 servings. You add only hot or cold water for reconstituting. The food is ready to serve without any heating or cooking. Studies at Utah State University indicate there is little loss of nutrition in freeze-dried foods stored 15 years. Freeze-dried foods should also be rotated, page 3.

Land-Locked Fish Chowder

White fish may be bass, sole, haddock, cod or scallops.

1 to 1-1/2 lbs. frozen white fish,
  partially thawed
2 medium potatoes, peeled, cubed
2 large carrots, sliced
4 cups water
1 small onion, chopped
2 tablespoons dried chopped green peppers
5 bacon slices

2 tablespoons all-purpose flour
2 cups milk
1/2 teaspoon seasoned salt
1/2 teaspoon pepper
Salt to taste
4 saltine crackers, broken
2 tablespoons butter or margarine

Cut fish into 1-inch squares. In a large saucepan, combine potatoes, carrots, water, fish pieces, onion and green peppers. Cover and bring to a boil. Cook over medium heat until vegetables are crisp-tender, about 15 minutes. While fish mixture cooks, sauté bacon in a medium skillet until browned and most of the fat is cooked out. Remove bacon from skillet. Stir flour into bacon fat until bubbly. Slowly stir in milk, seasoned salt, pepper and salt. Continue stirring over medium heat until mixture is smooth and slightly thickened. Crumble bacon. Reserve about 1 tablespoon crumbled bacon for garnish. Stir milk mixture and remaining crumbled bacon into fish mixture. Simmer 5 to 10 minutes longer. Stir cracker pieces and butter or margarine into chowder. Sprinkle with reserved crumbled bacon. Serve immediately. Makes 4 to 6 servings.

Split Pea & Lentil Soup

A special treat with hot rolls and a salad.

1 cup green split peas
1/2 cup lentils
4 cups cold water
1/2 cup pearl barley
2 tablespoons dried chopped onion
1 teaspoon salt

1/4 teaspoon pepper
1/4 teaspoon celery salt
1 to 2 cups water
Ham hock, pork bones or ham pieces
1 teaspoon dried leaf parsley

Combine split peas, lentils and 4 cups cold water in a medium saucepan. Bring to a boil over medium-high heat. Remove from heat. Let stand 1 hour. Stir in barley, onion, salt, pepper, celery salt and 1 cup water. Add ham hock, pork bones or ham pieces. Bring to a boil over medium-high heat again. Reduce heat so soup continues to simmer. Cook about 1-1/2 hours until split peas and lentils are tender. Add more water during cooking if you prefer a thinner soup. Ladle into a soup tureen. Sprinkle with parsley. Serve hot. Makes 6 to 8 servings.

Land-Locked Fish Chowder and French Bread, page 126

Root Cellar Soup

This hearty soup is equally good served hot or cold.

1-1/2 cups Homemade Chicken Broth,
    page 41, or canned chicken broth
1 bay leaf
1/8 teaspoon garlic powder
1 teaspoon celery salt
1/8 teaspoon pepper
1 teaspoon salt
3 carrots, cut in 1/2-inch slices

1/2 large onion, sliced
2 medium potatoes, peeled, diced
2 cups shredded cabbage
2 cups beet juice from canned beets
1 tablespoon cider vinegar
1 teaspoon sugar
1/4 cup Homemade Yogurt, page 18, or
    plain yogurt, if desired

Combine chicken broth, bay leaf, garlic powder, celery salt, pepper and salt in a medium saucepan. Add carrots, onion and potatoes. Bring to a boil; reduce heat. Cover and simmer 10 minutes. Place cabbage on top of vegetables. Cover and simmer 5 minutes longer. Add beet juice, vinegar and sugar; stir. Cover and bring to a boil. Remove from heat. Ladle into soup bowls. If desired, top each serving with a spoonful of yogurt. Makes 4 servings.

Black-Bean Soup

Black beans, popular in Latin America, are also called black turtle beans.

About 3 cups water
3 cups Homemade Chicken Broth, page 41,
    or canned chicken broth
1 tablespoon dried minced onion
1/2 teaspoon garlic powder
1/2 teaspoon ground coriander
1/4 teaspoon ground thyme

1/2 teaspoon dried leaf oregano, crushed
2 cups dried black beans, sorted, rinsed
4 bacon slices, chopped
2 teaspoons salt
1/4 cup dry sherry, if desired
About 1/4 cup chopped fresh onion,
    if desired

Combine water, chicken broth, dried onion, garlic powder, coriander, thyme and oregano in a large saucepan or pot. Bring to a boil. Drop in a handful of beans at a time, keeping cooking liquid at a rapid boil. Cover and remove from heat. Let stand 1 hour. Bring to a boil; reduce heat. Simmer covered 45 minutes. Add bacon. Simmer 30 to 45 minutes longer until beans are tender, adding more water as needed. Stir in salt and sherry, if desired. Simmer 10 minutes longer. Serve in soup bowls. Top each serving with a spoonful of chopped fresh onion, if desired. Makes 4 to 6 servings.

Variation

Substitute 1/2 to 1 pound ham hocks, ham shanks or pork cubes for the bacon.

How to Make Root Cellar Soup

1/Prepare vegetables for soup.

2/Top each serving with yogurt.

Cold Potato Soup

If you use a leek instead of an onion, call this soup vichyssoise.

1 large onion, chopped
2 tablespoons vegetable oil
1 cup water
2 chicken bouillon cubes
1 (5.33-oz.) can evaporated milk

2 cups milk
1 (1/2-oz.) pkg. butter-flavor granules
1 cup instant potato flakes
1 teaspoon dried chopped celery

Sauté onion in oil in a medium, heavy saucepan until tender; do not let brown. Add water and bouillon cubes. Bring to a boil, stirring occasionally to dissolve cubes. Remove from heat. Stir in evaporated milk, milk, butter-flavor granules and potato flakes. Let stand about 5 minutes. Pour into a blender and process until almost smooth; small pieces of onion will add texture. Stir in celery. Cover and refrigerate. Serve chilled. Makes 4 servings.

Variation

Hot Potato Soup: After blending, pour soup back into saucepan. Bring to serving temperature over medium heat, stirring occasionally. Ladle hot soup into individual soup bowls. Sprinkle each serving with dried chopped celery.

Mandarin Soup

A delightful appetizer or dessert soup!

1 (11-oz.) can mandarin orange segments
Water
1-1/2 tablespoons sugar
2 tablespoons cornstarch

2 tablespoons orange breakfast-drink powder
2 whole cloves
1-1/2 cups water
2 tablespoons lime juice

Drain mandarin orange segments, reserving juice. Add water to juice to make 1 cup. Combine juice mixture, sugar, cornstarch and orange drink powder in a medium saucepan. Stir until blended. Add cloves. Whisk constantly over medium-high heat until mixture is thickened. Gradually whisk in 1-1/2 cups water and heat to serving temperature. Remove cloves. Stir in orange segments and lime juice. Serve soup hot or cold. Makes 4 servings.

Sierra Vista Gazpacho

Top this cold Spanish soup with cucumber slices, minced onion or grated carrot.

1 (16-oz.) can tomatoes
2 cups vegetable juice cocktail
2 tablespoons wine vinegar
1/4 cup olive oil
2 tablespoons lime juice

1/2 teaspoon celery salt
1 teaspoon onion powder
1/8 teaspoon garlic powder
2 tablespoons canned chopped green chilies
1/4 cup croutons

Combine all ingredients except croutons in a blender. Process until smooth. Refrigerate at least 1 hour to chill. Top each serving with croutons. Makes 4 servings.

Variation

Stir in 1 cup chilled plain yogurt before serving.

Bargains

Sale items are not always wise buys for long-term storage. Some goods may already have been stored for a long time. This cancels their long-term storage value. Check each item you purchase for an expiration or *do-not-sell-after* date. If they are coded, ask the store manager for an interpretation.

Vegetables and fruits present the most difficult problems when living on stored foods. Unless you have a garden, fruit trees or a root cellar, fresh produce is not possible. Buy fresh fruits and vegetables as often as you can manage. They are less expensive in season and root vegetables are always a good buy.

Sprouted mung beans are by far the most practical storage item for providing freshness, crisp texture and vitamins. See page 8 for How to Sprout Mung Beans. Wheat and alfalfa can also be sprouted. See page 96 for How to Sprout Wheat.

Most of the supplies you will buy for this section can be kept for a long time at room temperature. Opened mayonnaise or salad dressing, mustard, oils and juices store best in the refrigerator. Breadcrumbs, croutons and cracked wheat will survive at room temperature for a short time. To be safe for long-term storage, keep them in your freezer. Butter-flavor granules can be kept at room temperature. They are used to flavor vegetables. Use the granules to make Herbed Topping. Butter-flavor granules have no fat so cannot be used for sautéing or to add needed fat to your diet. When mixed with vegetable oil or water, they can be used as a substitute for melted butter.

If you have to rely on canned goods, be sure to have 1 or 2 cases of canned tomatoes. They are rich in vitamins and are useful for sauces, soups, casseroles and stews. Although canned water chestnuts are a bit expensive, they are almost worth their weight in gold when you're living on stored foods. Their crisp texture adds needed crunch to salads and casseroles. You may use a dozen or more cans in a few months. Water chestnuts are available both sliced and whole.

A large freezer is not necessary to store foods for vegetable dishes and salads. If you have a small freezer, use it to best advantage for butter or margarine and cheese. Frozen vegetables used in the recipes in this section are relatively few. They include corn, peas, green beans, brussels sprouts and chopped broccoli.

Although canned vegetables and fruits have less nutritive value than frozen, you can maintain a balanced diet. As frequently as possible, add fresh vegetables or fresh sprouts and occasional fruit from the supermarket or a garden.

Some people may object to canned foods because of their high salt and sugar content. With this in mind, we have reduced salt and sugar in most of the recipes in this book calling for canned foods. You can reduce your salt and sugar intake even further by adding less than the recipes suggest.

Canned fruits and vegetables are better than none at all. We recommend you find a balance

Vegetables & Salads

between fresh, frozen and canned produce that suits your life-style, storage space and budget.

Adventurous cooks need a variety of herbs, spices and special ingredients to make mealtime an exciting and creative experience. These ingredients take up a minimum of space.

Dried shredded carrots, sometimes called dried carrot flakes, can add marvelous flavor and color to plain dishes. You can dry your own, page 9, using carrots from your garden or from the supermarket.

Malaysian Buffet

Singapore Salad, page 54
Tabbouleh, page 56
Sweet & Sour Chicken Wings, page 33
Beef Sate, page 84
Rice
Pita Bread
Gingerbread, page 118, with
English Lemon Curd, page 25
Frozen Melon Balls
Apple Juice

Mushroom Ramekins

Tender mushrooms baked in a savory sauce.

1 cup beef broth or bouillon
2 tablespoons dried minced onion
2 tablespoons cornstarch
1/8 teaspoon garlic powder
1/8 teaspoon ground thyme
1/8 teaspoon pepper

1 (8-oz.) can mushroom stems and pieces,
  drained
2 tablespoons sherry, if desired
4 teaspoons butter or margarine
1/4 cup soft breadcrumbs
4 teaspoons grated Parmesan cheese

Combine broth or bouillon and onion in a medium saucepan. Let stand 10 to 15 minutes to rehydrate onion. Combine cornstarch, garlic powder, thyme and pepper in a small bowl. Stir about 2 tablespoons rehydrated onion and broth into cornstarch mixture. Stir cornstarch mixture into onion mixture. Add mushrooms. Cook and stir over medium heat until mixture thickens. Preheat oven to 350F (175C). Remove mushroom mixture from heat. Stir in sherry, if desired. Divide mixture equally among four 1-cup ramekins or custard cups. Dot surface of each with 1 teaspoon butter or margarine. Sprinkle each with 1 tablespoon breadcrumbs and 1 teaspoon Parmesan cheese. Bake about 10 minutes until bubbly. Makes 4 servings.

Corn & Asparagus Scallop

Asparagus spears add a luxurious touch, yet they are economical.

1 (16-oz.) can whole-kernel corn
1 (14-1/2-oz.) can asparagus spears
1/2 cup evaporated milk
2 tablespoons butter or margarine

2 tablespoons all-purpose or
  whole-wheat flour
1/4 teaspoon celery salt
1 teaspoon dried leaf parsley

Drain corn and asparagus separately, reserving liquid. Add enough vegetable liquid to evaporated milk to make 1-1/2 cups. Melt butter or margarine in a medium saucepan over medium heat. Stir in flour until blended and bubbly. Gradually stir in milk mixture. Cook and stir until mixture is smooth and slightly thickened. Stir in celery salt. Preheat oven to 350F (175C). Spread drained corn over bottom of a 12" x 7-1/2" baking pan or a shallow 1-1/2-quart casserole. Arrange drained asparagus spears side-by-side over corn. Pour white sauce over center of asparagus spears. Sprinkle with parsley. Bake about 20 minutes until bubbly. Makes about 6 servings.

Use cooking liquid from vegetables to reconstitute dried eggs when the flavor will be compatible.

Instant Potato Boats

Onion, allspice and cheese make these baked potatoes unusual.

1 cup water
1/2 teaspoon salt
1 tablespoon butter or margarine
1/4 cup evaporated milk
1 tablespoon dried minced onion

1/8 teaspoon ground allspice
1/2 (5-oz.) pkg. instant potato flakes (1-1/4 cups)
1/2 cup shredded Cheddar cheese (2 oz.)
Paprika

Cut four 8" x 6" pieces heavy-duty foil. On each piece of foil, fold down 1 inch on all sides. Fold up about 1 inch at a 90° angle on 2 long sides. Fold 2 ends together. Corners will come together to form points. Set aside. Bring water to a boil in a medium saucepan. Pour water into a warm medium bowl. Stir in salt, butter or margarine, evaporated milk, onion and allspice. Add potato flakes, stirring only to moisten. Let stand 5 minutes. Preheat oven to 400F (205C). Stir potato mixture lightly with a fork. Spoon potato mixture into foil boats. Sprinkle tops with cheese and paprika. Place on a baking sheet. Bake 3 to 5 minutes until cheese melts. Serve immediately. Makes 4 servings.

How to Make Instant Potato Boats

1/Fold down 1 inch on all sides of foil rectangles. Fold up 1 inch at a 90° angle on 2 long sides. Fold ends together making boats.

2/Spoon potato mixture into foil boats. Sprinkle tops with shredded cheese.

Broccoli & Carrot Medley

Serve with Polka-Dot Bread, page 103.

2 (10-oz.) pkgs. frozen broccoli spears
2 (10-oz.) pkgs. frozen sliced carrots or
  2 (16-oz.) cans sliced carrots
1 tablespoon butter or margarine
3 tablespoons all-purpose flour

1/4 teaspoon salt
1-1/2 cups milk
1 cup shredded Longhorn cheese (4 oz.)
1/2 cup dry breadcrumbs

In 2 medium saucepans, cook broccoli and frozen carrots separately in water according to package directions; drain vegetables and set aside. If using canned carrots, drain and reserve liquid; use liquid as desired. Melt butter or margarine in a medium saucepan over low heat. Stir in flour and salt to a smooth paste. Stir in milk. Cook and stir until thickened, about 3 minutes. Preheat oven to 350F (175C). Arrange broccoli and carrots alternately in a 3-quart casserole. Pour white sauce over vegetables. Sprinkle top with cheese and breadcrumbs. Bake 10 minutes or until cheese melts and sauce bubbles. Serve immediately. Makes 4 to 6 servings.

Vegetable Quartet

An easy, make-ahead salad to add color to your table.

2 tablespoons vegetable oil
1 tablespoon cider vinegar
1/2 teaspoon dried leaf oregano, crushed
1/4 teaspoon dried dill weed
1/4 teaspoon salt
1/8 teaspoon pepper

1 (7-oz.) can whole-kernel corn,
  drained
1 (4-1/2-oz.) can ripe olives
1 (10-oz.) pkg. frozen peas, cooked
1 (16-oz.) can tomatoes, chopped, drained

In a small jar with a tight-fitting lid, combine oil, vinegar, oregano, dill weed, salt and pepper. Shake to blend. Combine corn, olives, peas and tomatoes in a serving bowl. Toss gently to mix. Refrigerate until ready to serve. Pour dressing over vegetables before serving. Toss gently. Makes 4 or 5 servings.

Frozen Foods

Frozen foods thaw rapidly. Select them just before going through the checkout and go directly home to place frozen items in the freezer. If you plan to buy in quantity, contact the store manager and request cases be ordered for you.

Shown on the shelves starting from the top, Spicy Beet Bread, page 128; Polka-Dot Bread, page 103; frozen limes, page 11; Freezer Red Raspberry Jam, page 25; and water-glass eggs, page 13.

Singapore Salad

Serve this salad in a pretty oriental bowl.

1 (15-1/4-oz.) can pineapple chunks,
  drained
1 (11-oz.) can mandarin orange segments,
  drained
1 (4-oz.) can sliced water chestnuts,
  drained

1/2 cup cooked frozen peas
1-1/2 tablespoons lime juice
1/4 teaspoon salt
1/4 cup fresh mung bean sprouts,
  if desired

Combine pineapple, mandarin orange segments, water chestnuts and peas in a medium bowl. Sprinkle with lime juice and salt. Mix gently. Refrigerate until ready to serve. Sprinkle sprouts over top of salad before serving, if desired. Makes 4 servings.

Potato Salad Platter

The perfect picnic salad for healthy appetites!

1 (16-oz.) can fingerling carrots
1 (15-oz.) can sliced potatoes
2 tablespoons chopped fresh onion
1/4 cup mayonnaise
2 teaspoons cider vinegar
1 teaspoon olive oil

1 teaspoon dry mustard
1/4 teaspoon garlic powder
1/4 teaspoon celery salt
Dash of pepper
1 (5-oz.) can Vienna sausages
1 (6-oz.) jar artichoke hearts

Slice about one-third of the carrots into a medium bowl. Add potatoes and onion. Combine mayonnaise, vinegar, olive oil, dry mustard, garlic powder, celery salt and pepper in a small bowl; mix well. Stir half the dressing into potato mixture. Mound potato mixture on a platter. Arrange Vienna sausages, artichoke hearts and remaining carrots around potato mixture. Serve remaining dressing separately for dipping sausages and carrots. Makes 4 servings.

Herb Seasoning

Sprinkle a little on your salad or soup.

1 tablespoon dried dill weed
1 tablespoon dried leaf oregano, crushed
1 tablespoon ground rubbed sage

1-1/2 teaspoons ground thyme
1 tablespoon ground coriander
1-1/2 teaspoons garlic powder

Combine all ingredients in a jar with a tight-fitting lid. Cover and shake to mix. Shake or stir again before using. Makes about 1/4 cup.

Singapore Salad and Fried Rice, page 59

Orange Fruit Molds

If you don't have 1/2-cup molds, use one 4-cup mold.

1 (16-oz.) can seedless grapes
1 (11-oz.) can mandarin orange segments
About 1 cup water
1 (3-oz.) pkg. orange-flavored gelatin

1 tablespoon orange breakfast-drink powder
1 cup cold water
1/2 cup walnut pieces
Mayonnaise, if desired

Drain grapes and mandarin orange segments, reserving juice. Refrigerate fruit. Add water to juice to make 2 cups. Bring mixture to a boil in a small saucepan. Remove from heat. Stir in gelatin and orange drink powder until dissolved. Pour into a medium bowl. Add 1 cup cold water; mix well. Refrigerate until partially set. Stir in fruit and walnuts. Spoon into eight 1/2-cup molds. Refrigerate until completely set. To unmold, invert each mold and shake lightly over a plate. Top with mayonnaise, if desired. Makes 8 servings.

Tabbouleh

You can make your own bulghur or buy it in health-food stores or some supermarkets.

1 cup bulghur, page 97
1-1/3 cups cold water
1/4 cup olive oil
2 to 3 tablespoons cider vinegar
3 to 4 tablespoons lime or lemon juice
2 tablespoons dried shredded carrot

3 tablespoons dried minced onion
3 tablespoons dried leaf parsley
1 tablespoon dried chopped mint
1/4 cup raisins
1/2 teaspoon salt
3 canned tomatoes, chopped, drained

Combine bulghur and cold water in a medium bowl. Let stand 20 minutes. Stir in remaining ingredients except tomatoes. Cover and refrigerate at least 2 hours. Before serving, stir in tomatoes. Makes 4 servings.

Vegetable Flake Dressing

Add spices and herbs according to your taste.

1 tablespoon dried chopped celery
1 tablespoon dried leaf parsley
1 tablespoon mixed dried chopped peppers
1 tablespoon dried shredded carrot
1 tablespoon dried minced onion

3 tablespoons water
3 tablespoons vegetable oil
3 tablespoons cider vinegar
1/2 teaspoon salt

Combine all ingredients in a small bowl. Let stand at room temperature 30 minutes. Stir before serving. Makes about 1/2 cup.

Bacon & Bean Curd Topping

Canned or frozen vegetables make perfect flavor and texture partners for browned bean curd.

3 (2-inch) squares Bean Curd, page 8
1/4 lb. bacon slices, diced

1/2 small onion, diced

Cut each bean curd square into 12 cubes. Heat a medium skillet over medium heat. Cook bacon in hot skillet until almost crisp, stirring frequently and reducing heat if necessary. Remove all but about 2 tablespoons bacon drippings from skillet; reserve for another use. Add onion and bean curd cubes to bacon. Reduce heat to low. Gently turn bean curd cubes as they cook to brown all sides. Remove from skillet and serve immediately. Makes about 1 cup.

Variation

Bean Curd Croutons: Omit onions. Substitute 2 to 3 tablespoons bacon drippings for bacon. Brown bean curd cubes in hot bacon drippings until crisp. Use immediately in soup or salad.

How to Make Bacon & Bean Curd Topping

1/Dice bacon and onion. Cut each bean curd square into 12 cubes.

2/Use sautéed bean curd mixture as a topping for vegetables.

Rice, pasta and dried beans are nutritious, satisfying foods that need few storage considerations. The most important points are to keep them clean and dry and use them on a rotating basis.

The main meal of the day doesn't have to be soup, meat, salad and vegetables, followed by dessert. One-dish meals with a salad or vegetable can be equally satisfying. An occasional rich dessert will be enjoyed after a lighter meal. Begin with Skillet Supper and Corn & Asparagus Scallop or Bean Tostadas with Orange Fruit Molds.

Rice and pasta are good sources of valuable vitamins and carbohydrates. The variation for

Rice, Pasta & Beans

Fettucini Alfredo with noodles, homemade yogurt and tuna provides an economical and nourishing meal.

Cooked dried beans and peas are good sources of protein. This protein is incomplete, which means it does not contain all the required amino acids. Grains such as wheat, corn and rice have those acids. They are called complementary proteins because when one of them is combined with a serving of beans or peas, together they make a complete protein. Complete proteins are in meat, eggs and cheese. For this reason a little meat or cheese is often added to beans.

Soybeans are the most nutritious of the legumes. They have been a staple in the Orient for centuries. Be experimental and try making your own bean curd, or *tofu*, from soybeans, see page 8.

The secret for getting as much flavor and nutrition as possible from rice, pasta and legumes is to stock up on compatible ingredients. Freeze meat and cheese in small 1/4-pound and 1/2-pound packets. Store small cans of ham, tuna, chicken, shrimp and beef. Our recipe for Hoppin' John is an example of one of these successful flavor combinations.

Split peas, lentils and soybeans will be quite savory when you stir in some exotic spices. You'll discover this when you try Split Peas Punjabi-Style and Cinnamon Soybeans.

With these recipes, your own ingenuity can shine. Use liquid from cooking vegetables or broth when you cook rice or beans. Try cooking rice or pasta in orange juice for a refreshing flavor. Substitutions can add a little variation. Many of these recipes call for a little juice drained from canned tomatoes. Use tomato juice, or dilute tomato sauce or barbecue sauce with water. Experiment with dried chopped vegetables. Stir leftover vegetables into a rice or macaroni salad. Cooking beans? Tuck some bacon, salt pork, or ham hocks in with them while they simmer and the flavor will improve dramatically.

Buy beans in 10- or 25-pound sacks and store them in several large storage containers or 5-pound coffee tins. Be sure to date the containers and keep them in a cool, dry place. Cook beans from your supply at least once a week. Beans kept longer than 10 years may be a little tough or have papery skins no matter how long you cook them.

4th of July Backyard Picnic

Corn Bread Pie, page 91
Cinnamon Soybeans, page 67
Vegetable Quartet, page 53
Bacon Biscuits, page 121
Independence Day Tartlets, page 145

Nottingham Rice Salad

An unusual and appealing main-dish salad.

1 cup uncooked long-grain rice
2 cups water
1/2 teaspoon salt
1 teaspoon olive oil
1/4 cup vegetable oil
1/4 cup cider vinegar

2 teaspoons dried leaf parsley
1/2 teaspoon celery salt
1 cup drained pickle chips, chilled
1 (6-1/2-oz.) can tuna, drained
1/3 cup coarsely chopped or broken walnuts

In a medium saucepan with a tight-fitting lid, combine rice, water, salt and olive oil. Bring to a boil. Reduce heat to low. Cover and cook about 20 minutes until water is absorbed. Combine vegetable oil, vinegar, parsley and celery salt in a small jar with a tight-fitting lid. Cover and shake to mix well. Pour over hot rice. Stir gently to mix well; set aside uncovered to cool. Refrigerate cooled rice until ready to serve. Cut about half the pickle chips in half and flake tuna. Stir halved pickle chips, flaked tuna and walnuts into rice before serving. Spoon onto a small platter. Garnish with whole pickle chips. Makes 4 to 6 servings.

Fried Rice   *Photo on page 55.*

Almost any sliced cooked meat or vegetable can be stirred in after the egg is added.

1 (6-oz.) pkg. frozen pea pods,
  cooked, drained
2 tablespoons freeze-dried or drained
  canned sliced mushrooms
2 tablespoons water for freeze-dried
  mushrooms
2 tablespoons vegetable oil
1/2 medium onion, chopped

2 cups cooked rice
1/2 cup frozen peas, partially thawed
1 egg, beaten, or equivalent
1 (8-oz.) can sliced water chestnuts
3 tablespoons soy sauce
2 oz. sliced salami, if desired
Additional soy sauce, if desired

Arrange cooked pea pods around the edge of a small platter; keep warm. Combine freeze-dried mushrooms and 2 tablespoons water in a small bowl. Let stand about 3 minutes to rehydrate mushrooms; drain. Preheat a large skillet over medium heat about 1 minute. Pour in oil; heat about 30 seconds. Sauté onion in hot oil until softened but not browned. Stir in rice and peas, breaking up any lumps of rice. When rice is hot, drizzle with beaten egg; stir. When no trace of moist egg remains, add water chestnuts, 3 tablespoons soy sauce, rehydrated or canned mushrooms and salami, if desired. Stir to mix well. Arrange on platter in center of pea pods. Serve immediately with additional soy sauce, if desired. Makes 4 servings.

Hoppin' John

Rice and beans are combined to make a hearty dish.

5 cups water
1-1/2 cups dried black-eyed peas
1 tablespoon dried chopped onion
1/4 teaspoon garlic powder
1 teaspoon salt
1/8 teaspoon pepper

3/4 cup uncooked long-grain rice
1/4 teaspoon ground savory
1 (1/2-oz.) pkg. butter-flavor granules
1 (6-1/2-oz.) can chunked and ground ham
Hot pepper sauce or barbecue sauce,
    if desired

Bring water to a boil in a medium saucepan. Sort and rinse peas. Drop peas into boiling water, maintaining a rolling boil. Add onion, garlic powder, salt and pepper. Reduce heat. Cover and simmer about 45 minutes until peas are almost tender. Stir in rice, savory and butter-flavor granules. Use 2 forks to flake ham or cut into cubes with a knife. Add to peas and rice mixture. Bring to a boil. Reduce heat. Cover and simmer until all liquid is absorbed and rice is tender, about 20 minutes. Serve hot. If desired, serve hot pepper sauce or barbecue sauce separately. Makes 6 to 8 servings.

Variation

Campers' Hoppin' John: Omit hot pepper sauce or barbecue sauce. Measure peas into a food-storage bag. Combine dried chopped onion, garlic powder, salt and pepper in a plastic sandwich bag. Secure with a twist tie. Combine rice and savory in another plastic sandwich bag. Add a dash of red (cayenne) pepper, if desired. Secure with a twist tie. Place both sandwich bags and butter-flavor granules package in the food-storage bag with the peas. Store with ham and a measuring cup. Cook as directed.

Brown Rice & Raisins

Make this hearty side dish even more nutritious by topping it with Homemade Yogurt, page 18.

2-1/2 cups water
1/2 teaspoon salt
1 cup uncooked brown rice
1/3 cup raisins
1 tablespoon dried minced onion

1 tablespoon dried leaf parsley
1/8 teaspoon ground savory
1/8 teaspoon ground cinnamon
1 (1/2-oz.) pkg. butter-flavor granules

In a medium saucepan with a tight-fitting lid, bring water to a boil. Add salt, rice, raisins, onion, parsley, savory and cinnamon. Reduce heat to low. Cover and cook about 50 minutes until water is absorbed. Stir in butter-flavor granules. Serve hot. Makes 6 servings.

Variation

Campers' Brown Rice & Raisins: Combine salt, brown rice, raisins, dried chopped onion, parsley, savory and cinnamon in a food-storage bag. Store with butter-flavor granules package and a measuring cup. Cook as directed.

How to Make Hoppin' John

1/Stir rice, savory and butter-flavor granules into bean mixture.

2/Use 2 forks to flake ham.

Fettucini Alfredo

Economical and low in calories.

1 (8-oz.) pkg. fettucini or spaghetti
Boiling salted water
1 tablespoon vegetable oil
1 cup Homemade Yogurt, page 18, or
    plain yogurt

1 (1/2-oz.) pkg. butter-flavor granules
1/2 teaspoon salt
1/4 teaspoon pepper
1/4 cup grated Parmesan cheese
1 teaspoon dried leaf parsley, if desired

Cook fettucini or spaghetti in boiling salted water with 1 tablespoon vegetable oil according to package directions. While pasta is cooking, heat yogurt over low heat in a small saucepan. Stir in butter-flavor granules, salt, pepper and Parmesan cheese. Rinse pasta quickly in cold water and drain. Turn out onto a platter. Pour yogurt mixture over pasta. Sprinkle with parsley, if desired. Serve immediately. Makes 4 to 6 servings.

Variation

Substitute broad egg noodles for fettucini or spaghetti. Break up 1 (6-1/2-ounce) can drained tuna and add to yogurt mixture before pouring over pasta.

Vegetable Lasagne

The flavor is even better on the second day after this is made.

4 cups Mediterranean Sauce, below
1 (8-oz.) pkg. lasagne noodles
Boiling salted water
1 tablespoon vegetable oil
2 cups shredded mozzarella cheese (8 oz.)
1 (16-oz.) container ricotta cheese
3 egg whites or equivalent

1 (9-oz.) pkg. frozen Italian-style
    green beans, partially thawed
1 (10-oz.) pkg. frozen sliced carrots,
    partially thawed
1 (16-oz.) can Italian-style zucchini
1 (4-oz.) can mushrooms, drained
1/2 cup grated Parmesan cheese

Prepare Mediterranean Sauce. Lightly butter a 13'' x 9'' baking pan. Cook lasagne noodles in boiling salted water with 1 tablespoon oil according to package directions. Drain noodles in a colander. Rinse with cold water and drain again. Preheat oven to 375F (190C). In a medium bowl, mix mozzarella cheese, ricotta cheese and egg whites. In a large bowl, mix green beans, carrots, zucchini, mushrooms and Mediterranean Sauce. Spread one-fourth of the vegetable mixture over bottom of baking pan. Arrange one-third of the noodles across sauce. Top with one-third of the cheese mixture dropped by small spoonfuls. Repeat layers starting and ending with vegetable mixture. Sprinkle with Parmesan cheese. Bake lasagne 25 minutes. Let stand 5 minutes before serving. Cut into squares to serve. Makes 8 to 10 servings.

Mediterranean Sauce

Tasty sauce for spaghetti or lasagne or to top meat loaf or chicken.

2 (16-oz.) cans tomatoes, chopped
1 (16-oz.) can stewed tomatoes
1 (12-oz.) can tomato paste
1 (15-oz.) can tomato sauce
1 tablespoon brown sugar
1-1/2 teaspoons dried leaf oregano
1 teaspoon dried leaf basil, crushed

1 teaspoon ground allspice
1/2 teaspoon garlic powder
1 teaspoon fennel seeds, crushed
1 tablespoon dried minced onion
1 tablespoon mixed dried chopped peppers
1 tablespoon dried chopped celery
1/3 cup red wine, if desired

Combine all ingredients in a large saucepan. Bring to a boil over medium heat; reduce heat. Cover and cook over very low heat 1-1/2 hours, stirring occasionally. If sauce is too thin, remove cover and simmer 30 minutes longer. Cool before freezing. Pour into 1-cup or 2-cup freezer containers. Store in freezer up to 3 months. Makes 5 to 6 cups.

Marta's Macaroni & Cheese

An easy, inexpensive top-of-the-stove casserole from El Salvador.

2 cups elbow macaroni
Boiling salted water
1 tablespoon vegetable oil
1 (16-oz.) can tomatoes
2 teaspoons dried minced onion
1/4 teaspoon ground cumin

1/2 teaspoon ground coriander
1/2 teaspoon salt
1/8 teaspoon pepper
2 tablespoons olive oil
3/4 cup Cheddar cheese powder or shredded
    Cheddar or Monterey Jack cheese

Cook macaroni in boiling salted water with 1 tablespoon vegetable oil according to package directions. Rinse in cold water; drain and set aside. Drain tomatoes, reserving liquid. Chop tomatoes. Add onion, cumin, coriander, salt and pepper to reserved tomato liquid; stir. Return macaroni to saucepan. Toss with olive oil. Stir in chopped tomatoes, tomato liquid mixture and cheese powder or shredded cheese; mix well. Cover and bring to serving temperature over medium heat, stirring frequently. Makes 4 to 6 servings.

Skillet Supper

An economical supper you can serve with pride.

Breakfast Sausage, page 26, uncooked
1 (8-oz.) pkg. egg noodles
Boiling salted water
1 teaspoon vegetable oil

3 medium onions, halved
1/2 to 1 cup Homemade Yogurt, page 18,
    or plain yogurt

Prepare Breakfast Sausage. Preheat a large skillet over medium heat. Brown sausage in skillet, stirring with a spatula to break up meat. Cook noodles in boiling salted water with 1 teaspoon oil according to package directions. Rinse in cold water and drain. While noodles are cooking, slice onion halves lengthwise. Add to skillet with sausage. Cook until onions are tender, stirring occasionally. Add drained cooked noodles to sausage mixture. Stir to mix well. Top each serving with yogurt. Makes 4 servings.

Variation

TVP Skillet: Pour 1/2 cup chicken broth or bouillon over 1/2 cup chicken-flavor TVP granules. Let stand 10 to 15 minutes to rehydrate TVP granules. Make half the amount of recipe for Breakfast Sausage. Brown sausage. Add rehydrated TVP granules to sausage with onions. Stir in 1 teaspoon soy sauce before adding noodles. If mixture is dry, stir in 1/2 cup chicken broth or bouillon.

Hard cheeses freeze and thaw with very little change in their texture or flavor; see page 10.

Curried Chicken Salad

Delicious make-ahead, confetti-colored salad.

1 cup ditalini noodles
Boiling salted water
1 teaspoon vegetable oil
1 (10-oz.) pkg. cooked frozen
   mixed vegetables
1 (6-3/4-oz.) can chunked and
   ground chicken

1/4 to 1/2 cup mayonnaise
3 tablespoons milk
1/2 teaspoon salt
1/4 teaspoon curry powder
1/4 teaspoon poultry seasoning
1/4 cup finely chopped fresh onion

Cook ditalini in boiling salted water with 1 teaspoon oil according to package directions. Rinse in cold water; drain and refrigerate. Refrigerate cooked vegetables. Shred chicken meat with 2 forks, mixing liquid into meat. Combine 1/4 cup mayonnaise, milk, salt, curry powder and poultry seasoning in a small bowl. Combine shredded chicken, onion, noodles, vegetables and curry mixture in a large bowl; mix well. Refrigerate until ready to serve. Stir to mix before serving. Add more mayonnaise, if desired. Makes 4 or 5 servings.

Split Peas Punjabi-Style

Serve these with your favorite curry or scoop them up with wedges of pita bread.

1-1/2 cups dried split peas
3-1/2 cups water, Homemade Chicken Broth,
   page 41, or canned chicken broth
1 (1/2-oz.) pkg. butter-flavor granules
1 teaspoon salt
1/2 teaspoon ground cumin
1 teaspoon ground turmeric

1/8 teaspoon ground cinnamon
1/4 teaspoon red (cayenne) pepper
1/4 teaspoon ground ginger
1/4 teaspoon ground coriander
1/4 teaspoon dry mustard
1/8 teaspoon ground cloves

Rinse split peas in cold water. Combine split peas and 3-1/2 cups water or chicken broth in a medium saucepan. Bring to a boil; reduce heat. Cover and simmer until peas are very soft and broth has thickened, about 1 hour. Remove from heat. Stir in remaining ingredients. Cover and let stand 5 to 10 minutes to let flavors develop. Makes 6 to 8 servings.

Variations

Campers' Split Peas Punjabi-Style: Measure split peas into a food-storage bag. Use 1 bouillon cube to make broth. Combine salt, cumin, turmeric, cinnamon, red pepper, ginger, coriander, mustard and cloves in a plastic sandwich bag. Secure with a twist tie. Place bouillon cube, butter-flavor granules package and sandwich bag in the food-storage bag with the split peas. Store with a measuring cup. Cook as directed.

Substitute lentils for the split peas.

Angell's Vegetable Loaf

Every bit as good as a meat loaf.

1 (16-oz.) can carrots
1 (16-oz.) can green beans
1-1/2 cups cooked dried lima beans or
    pinto beans
3 cups dry breadcrumbs
2 tablespoons bacon drippings or
    vegetable oil
1 tablespoon dried leaf parsley

1/2 cup chili sauce
1 egg, beaten, or equivalent
2 tablespoons dried chopped onion
1/4 teaspoon celery salt
1/8 teaspoon pepper
2 bacon slices
Chili sauce or ketchup

Drain carrots and green beans, reserving liquid. In a food processor, food grinder or blender, process or grind drained carrots, green beans and lima beans or pinto beans a little at a time until almost smooth. Pour into a large bowl. Stir in breadcrumbs, bacon drippings or oil, parsley, 1/2 cup chili sauce, egg, onion, celery salt and pepper. Stir to blend. Stir in reserved vegetable liquid 1/4 cup at a time until mixture holds together. Preheat oven to 350F (175C). Grease a 9" x 5" loaf pan. Spoon vegetable mixture into loaf pan. Press into a compact loaf. Arrange bacon slices lengthwise over top of loaf. Bake 30 to 45 minutes until lightly browned. Serve with additional chili sauce or ketchup. Makes 5 servings.

African Shrimp Salad

Black-eyed peas, or cowpeas, have nourished generations in the southern United States.

1 cup dried black-eyed peas
About 3 cups water
2 tablespoons vegetable oil
1 tablespoon lime juice or lemon juice
3 tablespoons tomato juice
1 tablespoon cider vinegar

2 canned whole tomatoes, chopped
2 teaspoons dried minced onion
1/4 teaspoon garlic powder
5 or 6 bacon slices
1 (4-1/2-oz.) can tiny shrimp, drained

Sort and rinse peas. Bring water to a boil in a medium saucepan. Add 1 tablespoon oil and peas. Return to a boil; reduce heat. Cover and simmer 1 to 1-1/2 hours until tender, adding more water as needed to keep peas covered. Drain well and refrigerate. Combine 1 tablespoon oil, lime or lemon juice, tomato juice, vinegar and tomatoes in a small bowl. Stir in onion and garlic powder; set aside. Heat a medium skillet over medium heat. Dice bacon. Cook over low heat in skillet, stirring frequently to cook on all sides and removing fat from skillet as needed. Remove bacon from skillet and drain on paper towels. Add tomato mixture and shrimp to chilled peas. Toss to mix. Refrigerate until ready to serve. Before serving, sprinkle with cooked bacon. Makes 4 servings.

Variation

Substitute 1 (15-ounce) can garbanzo beans, drained, for the cooked black-eyed peas.

How to Make Angell's Vegetable Loaf

1/Combine ingredients in a large bowl.

2/Press mixture into loaf pan. Top with bacon slices.

Cinnamon Soybeans

Enjoy this tempting side dish at your next cookout.

2 cups dried soybeans, sorted, rinsed
1 cinnamon stick
6 cups water
1 tablespoon vegetable oil

1/4 cup packed brown sugar
1/4 cup cider vinegar
1/3 cup molasses
2 teaspoons salt

Soak soybeans in water to cover 8 to 12 hours. Drain; discard water and remove loose skins. Combine soaked soybeans, cinnamon stick, 6 cups water and oil in a large saucepan. Bring to a boil. Reduce heat to low. Skim off foam and bean skins that rise to the surface. Partially cover saucepan. Simmer 3 hours, adding more boiling water if necessary to keep soybeans covered. Drain soybeans, reserving cooking liquid. Stir brown sugar, vinegar, molasses, salt and 1 cup reserved cooking liquid into soybeans. Cover and simmer 30 minutes. Makes 6 to 8 servings.

Refried Beans   *Photo on page 29.*

Enjoy these beans with Poached Eggs Mexican-Style, page 28.

1 tablespoon bacon drippings
2 cups cooked or canned pinto beans or
   black beans

1 tablespoon cider vinegar
Salt, if desired

Heat bacon drippings in a medium skillet over medium heat. Add beans and mash with a potato masher. Mash in vinegar and salt, if desired. Cook, mashing and stirring frequently, until beans have a paste-like consistency. Serve hot. Makes 4 servings.

Carroll's Salsa

Bring a bit of Mexico to your dishes with this super salsa!

1 (16-oz.) can stewed tomatoes
1 medium onion, cut in quarters
1 (4-oz.) can chopped green chilies

1/2 teaspoon salt
1/4 teaspoon garlic powder
3 to 5 drops hot pepper sauce

Pour half the tomatoes into a blender. Add onion. Blend until onion is chopped fine. Add remaining tomatoes, chilies, salt, garlic powder and hot pepper sauce. Blend 2 to 4 seconds. Refrigerate in a tightly covered container. Makes about 2-1/2 cups.

Bacon Drippings

Whenever you cook bacon, pour the drippings into a tin can that has a lid. When the drippings cool, refrigerate them. They will keep for months. Brown meat for a stew or casserole in bacon drippings. Cook eggs in bacon drippings for a hearty flavor.

For long-term storage, buy 1 or 2 cases of your favorite seafood and 2 or 3 cans of each of the following: anchovies, clams, crab, mackerel, oysters, salmon, sardines and shrimp. These will be the basis of your fish or seafood meals.

Probably no canned fish or meat is as universally popular or has as many uses as tuna fish. It can be mixed with vegetables and dressings to make wonderful sandwich fillings and salads. Use it in skillet dishes, casseroles and chowders. Try Aspic Tuna Ring and Nottingham Rice Salad.

Canned chicken can be purchased whole, ground and chunked, boned and chunked, and pieces in gravy. Several canned whole chickens are invaluable for long-term storage. Each one is packed in a broth that can be used in the same recipe or in a separate soup or sauce. Ground and chunked chicken is especially good in salads and other dishes calling for small chicken pieces or shreds. Chicken pieces in gravy can be heated and served over toast or rice. Add vegetables and broth to create a soup or stew.

Frozen Chicken

Wrap chicken in freezer wrap or place it in freezer bags before freezing. Place 2 sheets of waxed paper between chicken pieces so they can be separated easily for thawing. The wrappings should be airtight. Poultry can be frozen 6 to 9 months. Wrap and freeze giblets separately. They will keep for 2 to 3 months. Chicken livers can be frozen only 1 month.

It's not necessary to rewrap whole turkeys because they are packaged in airtight moisture- and vapor-proof wrappings.

Thaw poultry in the refrigerator and cook it as soon as it thaws.

Do not freeze cooked or uncooked poultry you have stuffed at home. Cooking does not kill salmonella bacteria that tends to grow in stuffing. If the stuffed bird must be frozen, remove the stuffing first.

Frozen Fish

When you return from the supermarket or fish market, rewrap and freeze fresh fish immediately to preserve its fresh flavor. If you are returning from a fishing trip, clean and scale the fish right away. Place 2 sheets of waxed paper or freezer wrap between fish fillets. This allows easy separation after they are frozen. Wrap fish tightly in freezer wrap, gently pressing out air pockets.

Another excellent method of freezing fish is to freeze it in a block of ice. Clean fish and place the whole fish or fillets in a freezer container, foil pan or clean milk carton. Cover the fish with water, cover the container and freeze. When it is frozen solid, dip the container in warm water.

Or invert it and place a towel that has been dipped in hot water over the bottom and sides. Shake the loosened block of ice from the container. Place it in a freezer storage bag and secure with a twist tie. Label the bag and store it in the freezer. Allow time for thawing both the ice block and the fish before cooking.

Salt-water fish can be frozen by the same method in a solution of 4 teaspoons of salt to 1 quart of water.

Fresh, fatty or rich fish such as flounder, herring, lake trout, mackerel, pink salmon, ocean perch, shad, smelt and tuna can be frozen for 3 months. Lean fish such as cod, fresh-water herring, haddock, halibut, yellow perch, yellow pike and red salmon can be frozen for 6 months. Longer freezing causes loss of flavor and texture.

Thaw fish and seafood in the refrigerator. Thaw large whole fish and fish to be dipped in batter or crumbs. For other cooking methods, frozen fish can be cooked without being thawed. Cook fish when it's partially frozen or as soon as it is thawed. Do not refreeze it.

Weekend Fish Fry

Brunswick Stew

Buttermilk Corn Bread, page 128, adds the finishing touch to this single-dish meal.

1 whole (2-1/2- to 3-lb.) chicken
1 tablespoon bacon drippings or
 vegetable oil
1-1/2 cups water
1 (16-oz.) can stewed tomatoes
2 tablespoons dried minced onion
1 tablespoon dried leaf parsley
1 tablespoon mixed dried chopped peppers
1 tablespoon Worcestershire sauce

2 to 3 drops hot pepper sauce
1 tablespoon cider vinegar
1 teaspoon dry mustard
2 whole cloves
1 teaspoon salt
1 (16-oz.) can whole-kernel corn,
 undrained
1 (10-oz.) pkg. frozen baby lima beans

Rinse chicken; dry on paper towels. Heat bacon drippings or oil in a large pot or Dutch oven. Brown chicken on all sides in drippings or oil. Remove from heat. Add water, stewed tomatoes, onion, parsley, peppers, Worcestershire sauce, hot pepper sauce, vinegar, dry mustard, cloves and salt. Bring to a boil; reduce heat. Cover and simmer 45 to 55 minutes. Stir in corn and lima beans. Bring to a boil; reduce heat. Cover and simmer 15 minutes. Makes 5 or 6 servings.

Variation

Campers' Brunswick Stew: Omit bacon drippings or oil, Worcestershire sauce, hot pepper sauce and vinegar. Use 1 (3-pound 2-ounce) can whole chicken for chicken. Substitute 1 (16-ounce) can green lima beans, for the frozen lima beans. Combine onion, parsley, peppers, 1/8 teaspoon red (cayenne) pepper, dry mustard, cloves and salt in a plastic sandwich bag. Secure with a twist tie. Store until ready to use. To cook, drain chicken, reserving broth. Cut chicken into pieces. Remove skin, bones and fat; discard. Do not brown chicken. Combine reserved broth, tomatoes and ingredients of plastic bag in a large pot. Bring to a boil. Cover and simmer about 10 minutes. Add chicken, corn and lima beans. If stew is too thick, fill one of the empty vegetable cans with water and stir water into the stew. Cover and bring to a boil. Serve hot.

Crock-Pot Chicken & Broth

Start this in the morning when you need broth or chopped cooked chicken for dinner.

1 whole (2-1/2- to 3-lb.) chicken
3 cups water
1/2 teaspoon salt

1 tablespoon dried minced onion
1 tablespoon dried leaf parsley
1 tablespoon dried shredded carrot

Combine all ingredients in slow-cooker. Cook on low 4 to 6 hours, until meat has pulled away from bones. Remove chicken from broth. Remove bones and skin; discard. Chop chicken meat. Use broth for cooking rice or making soup. Makes about 3 cups of chopped chicken and about 1 quart of chicken broth.

Orange Chicken & Rice

Herbs and orange breakfast-drink powder give chicken and rice a glorious flavor.

1 (3-lb. 2-oz.) can whole chicken	**1 tablespoon dried minced onion**
Water	**1/8 teaspoon dried leaf thyme**
1 (1/2-oz.) pkg. butter-flavor granules	**1/2 teaspoon poultry seasoning**
2 tablespoons orange breakfast-drink	**1/2 teaspoon salt**
** powder**	**1/2 teaspoon grated orange peel**
1 cup uncooked long-grain rice	**Strips of orange peel for garnish**

Drain chicken, reserving broth. If necessary, add water to measure 2 cups. Remove skin, bones and fat from chicken; discard. Set chicken meat aside. Preheat oven to 400F (205C). Combine reserved broth, butter-flavor granules and orange drink powder. Stir to mix well. Place rice, onion, thyme, poultry seasoning, salt and grated orange peel in a 2-quart casserole. Stir to mix. Arrange chicken on top of rice mixture. Pour liquid mixture over chicken and rice. Cover and bake 30 to 45 minutes until liquid is absorbed and rice is tender. Remove from oven; let stand covered 10 minutes before serving. Garnish with strips of orange peel. Makes about 5 servings.

Variation

Campers' Orange Chicken & Rice: Use dried grated orange peel or orange peel granules. Combine butter-flavor granules and orange breakfast-drink powder in a small airtight container. Combine rice, onion, thyme, poultry seasoning, salt and orange peel in a food-storage bag. Store small container, plastic bag and canned chicken until ready to use. Cook as directed.

How to Make Orange Chicken & Rice

1/Discard skin, bones and fat from chicken.

2/Garnish finished dish with strips of orange peel.

Chicken Enchilada Bake

Serve this family favorite with a tossed salad.

1 (3-lb. 2-oz.) can whole chicken
Water
1 (4-oz.) can chopped green chilies
4 to 6 tablespoons dried minced onion
1 (10-3/4-oz.) can condensed cream of
   chicken soup

1/2 cup vegetable oil
12 corn tortillas
3 cups shredded Longhorn or
   Cheddar cheese (12 oz.)

Drain chicken, reserving broth. If necessary, add water to broth to measure 1-1/2 cups. Remove skin, bones and fat from chicken; discard. Chop chicken meat. In a large saucepan, combine chopped chicken, chilies, onion, soup and reserved broth. Bring to a simmer over medium heat. Simmer 3 to 5 minutes, stirring occasionally; do not boil. Remove sauce from heat and keep warm. Heat oil in a medium skillet to 365F (130C). At this temperature, a 1-inch cube of bread will turn golden brown in 50 to 60 seconds. With tongs, dip tortillas one at a time into hot oil. Quickly turn over, dipping other side in hot oil. Remove and place between layers of paper towels. Repeat until all tortillas have been dipped into hot oil. Preheat oven to 375F (190C). Cut or tear tortillas in half and line bottom of a 13" x 9" baking pan with one-third of the tortilla pieces. Do not overlap. Tear into smaller pieces if necessary. Cover with one-third of the heated sauce and 1 cup cheese. Make 2 more layers. Bake 20 to 25 minutes. Let stand 5 minutes before serving. Makes 4 to 6 servings.

Oven-Baked Chicken

Golden tender chicken with a superb flavor.

1 (3-lb.) chicken, cut in pieces
1/2 cup evaporated milk
1 tablespoon lemon juice
1 teaspoon Worcestershire sauce
1 teaspoon celery salt
1/2 teaspoon paprika

1/2 teaspoon dried minced garlic
1 teaspoon salt
Pinch of pepper
1 cup dry breadcrumbs
1/4 cup grated Parmesan cheese

Rinse chicken; dry on paper towels. Set aside. In a medium bowl, combine evaporated milk and lemon juice. Let stand 5 minutes until evaporated milk curdles. Preheat oven to 350F (175C). Grease a 13" x 9" baking pan. Stir Worcestershire sauce, celery salt, paprika, garlic, salt and pepper into curdled milk mixture. Place breadcrumbs and Parmesan cheese in a pie pan; mix well. Dip chicken pieces into milk mixture, coating all sides, then into breadcrumbs. Arrange coated chicken pieces in prepared baking pan. Bake about 50 minutes until chicken is golden brown and pulls apart easily when tested with a fork. Arrange chicken on a platter. Makes about 5 servings.

Chicken-Shrimp Curry in Parslied Rice

To plump raisins, combine equal amounts of raisins and boiling water, then let them cool.

Parslied Rice, see below
2 tablespoons butter or margarine
2 tablespoons all-purpose flour
2-1/2 to 2-3/4 cups milk
2 teaspoons instant chicken
**   bouillon granules**
1/4 teaspoon black pepper
1/4 teaspoon ground allspice
1 to 1-1/2 teaspoons curry powder

1 cup chopped cooked chicken or
**   1 (6-oz.) can boned chicken**
1 (4-1/2-oz.) can shrimp, drained,
**   deveined**
Mixed Fruit Chutney, page 145
1 (8-1/4-oz.) can pineapple chunks,
**   drained**
1/2 cup raisins, plumped, if desired
1/2 cup shredded coconut, if desired

Parslied Rice:
1-1/2 cups uncooked long-grain rice
3 cups cold water
1/2 teaspoon salt

1 tablespoon dried leaf parsley
3 tablespoons butter or margarine

Prepare Parslied Rice; keep warm. In a large skillet, melt butter or margarine over medium heat. Stir in flour until smooth and bubbly. Vigorously stir in 2-1/2 cups milk. Cook and stir until sauce is smooth and thickened. Stir in remaining 1/4 cup milk if needed to make a medium-thick sauce. Stir in bouillon granules, pepper, allspice and curry powder. Simmer 3 to 5 minutes over medium heat, stirring occasionally. Stir in chicken and shrimp. Spoon chutney and pineapple into 2 small serving bowls. If desired, spoon raisins and coconut into 2 other small serving bowls. Spoon hot rice around edge of a medium platter, making a ring. Turn curried mixture into center of rice ring. Serve with condiments. Makes about 6 servings.

Parslied Rice:
In a large saucepan with a tight-fitting lid, combine rice, cold water and salt. Bring to a boil over medium heat. Reduce heat to low. Cover and cook about 20 minutes until water is absorbed and rice is tender. Stir in parsley and butter or margarine.

Cutting up a whole chicken is easier when the chicken has been frozen and only partially thawed.

Chicken Mole

Mexico's classic dish is pronounced MOH-lay.

1 (3-lb. 2-oz.) can whole chicken
Water
3 tablespoons butter or margarine
2 tablespoons all-purpose flour
1/4 cup dried minced onion
1/4 teaspoon garlic powder
1/2 cup fine breadcrumbs
1/8 teaspoon ground cloves
1/2 teaspoon ground cinnamon
1/4 teaspoon almond extract
1/4 teaspoon anise seeds

1 to 2 tablespoons chili powder
2 teaspoons unsweetened cocoa powder
1 teaspoon sugar
1 (8-oz.) can tomato sauce
2 tablespoons vegetable oil
1 cup uncooked long-grain rice
2 cups water
1/2 teaspoon salt
2 tablespoons toasted sesame seeds,
  below

Drain chicken, reserving broth. If necessary, add water to broth to measure 3 cups. Remove skin, bones and fat from chicken; discard. Set chicken meat aside. Melt butter or margarine in a large saucepan over medium-low heat. Whisk in flour. Cook 1 minute; do not brown. Gradually stir in 3 cups reserved chicken broth. Add onion, garlic powder, breadcrumbs, cloves, cinnamon, almond extract, anise seeds, chili powder, cocoa powder, sugar and tomato sauce. Bring to a boil; reduce heat. Simmer uncovered until slightly thickened, 30 to 45 minutes, stirring occasionally. Stir in chicken; keep warm. Heat oil in a medium saucepan with a tight-fitting lid over medium heat. Add rice; stir to coat with oil. Stir frequently over medium-high heat until rice is golden. Remove saucepan from heat. Let cool slightly. Pour in 2 cups water. Add salt. Return to medium heat and bring to a boil. Reduce heat to low. Cover and cook until water is absorbed and rice is tender. Place 1 serving of rice on each plate. Top with a serving of hot chicken mixture. Sprinkle with sesame seeds. Makes 4 to 6 servings.

Variations

Donna's Mole: Substitute Crock-Pot Chicken & Broth, page 70, for the canned chicken and broth. Substitute carob powder for the cocoa powder and wheat germ for the breadcrumbs.

Catherine's Mole: Omit sugar and cinnamon. Increase chili powder to 3 tablespoons.

Toasting Sesame Seeds

To toast sesame seeds, spread them on a baking sheet. Bake them in a preheated 350F (175C) oven for about 10 minutes until they are golden. Watch them carefully and stir occasionally because the oil in the seeds causes them to burn easily. Cool the toasted seeds and use them immediately or store them in an airtight container.

Fish & Rings

On a lazy day, serve them with salt and ketchup.

Tartar Sauce, below, or Tangy
  Tomato Sauce, below
1 (16-oz.) pkg. frozen haddock fillets,
  partially thawed
1 small onion

Oil for deep-frying
1-1/2 cups all-purpose flour
1-1/2 cups carbonated lemon or lime soda
Salt to taste

Prepare Tartar Sauce or Tangy Tomato Sauce. Peel carton from fish. Cut down center of fish lengthwise. Cut fish crosswise into 6 or 7 pieces. Cut each piece in half. Cut onion into 1/4-inch slices. Pull slices apart into rings. Pour oil 1 inch deep in a heavy skillet or saucepan. Heat to 375F (190C). At this temperature, a 1-inch cube of bread will turn golden brown in 50 seconds. Mix flour and carbonated soda in a medium bowl. Dip fish pieces and onion rings in mixture to coat well. Lower a few fish pieces and rings at a time into hot oil with a slotted spoon. Fry until golden brown on all sides. Remove from oil with slotted spoon and drain on paper towels. Sprinkle with salt. Serve hot with Tartar Sauce or Tangy Tomato Sauce. Makes 4 to 6 servings.

Tartar Sauce

Traditionally served with fried fish but just as delicious on hamburgers!

2 tablespoons sweet relish
1/2 cup mayonnaise
1 to 2 tablespoons sweet pickle juice,
  if desired

1 teaspoon prepared mustard
1 teaspoon Worcestershire sauce

Combine all ingredients in a small bowl. Mix well. Refrigerate until ready to serve. Makes about 2/3 cup.

Tangy Tomato Sauce

Enjoy it with Fish & Rings, above.

1 tablespoon sweet relish
1/2 cup mayonnaise

2 tablespoons ketchup or chili sauce

Combine all ingredients in a small bowl. Mix well. Refrigerate until ready to serve. Makes about 2/3 cup.

Limed Fish & Rice

An unusual and delicious chilled fish salad.

1 cup uncooked long-grain rice
2 cups water
1/2 teaspoon salt
Pinch of dried leaf tarragon, crushed
1 teaspoon vegetable oil
2 tablespoons cider vinegar
1/4 cup vegetable oil
1 teaspoon dried chopped celery
1 teaspoon dried leaf parsley
1 teaspoon prepared mustard

1/2 to 1 teaspoon salt
1/4 teaspoon pepper
1 (16-oz.) pkg. frozen skinless fish
 fillets, partially thawed
Butter or margarine, if desired
1/4 cup chopped fresh onion
1 (16-oz.) can tomatoes, chopped, drained
1/4 cup lime juice
Ripe olives, if desired

In a medium saucepan with a tight-fitting lid, combine rice, water, 1/2 teaspoon salt, tarragon and 1 teaspoon oil. Bring to a boil. Reduce heat to low. Cover and cook about 20 minutes until water is absorbed and rice is tender. Cool; refrigerate. Combine vinegar, 1/4 cup oil, celery, parsley, mustard, 1/2 to 1 teaspoon salt and pepper in a small jar with a tight-fitting lid; shake well. Refrigerate. Separate fish fillets. Broil or bake with butter or margarine, if desired, according to package directions. Cool; flake with 2 forks. In a large salad bowl, combine cooked fish, chilled rice, onion and tomatoes. Pour dressing over rice mixture; mix gently. Refrigerate until thoroughly chilled, then serve. Sprinkle with lime juice before serving. Garnish with ripe olives, if desired. Makes 4 to 6 servings.

Creamed Anchovies & Zucchini

A light main dish prepared in minutes.

1 (2-oz.) can flat fillets of anchovies
1/2 cup water
1 cup frozen cut zucchini
2 tablespoons butter or margarine

3 tablespoons all-purpose flour
1 cup milk
1/4 teaspoon dried leaf parsley, crushed
Toast or crackers

Drain anchovies in a strainer. Rinse lightly under cold water and remove large bones. Set aside to drain. Bring 1/2 cup water to a boil. Add zucchini. Bring to a second boil; reduce heat. Cover and simmer 3 minutes. Remove from heat and drain. Melt butter or margarine in a medium saucepan over low heat. Stir in flour until mixture is smooth. Stir in milk. Continue to stir over medium-low heat until thickened. Add cooked zucchini, parsley and drained anchovies. Mix gently and heat through. Serve immediately on toast or crackers. Makes 2 or 3 servings.

As a substitute for fresh milk, use reconstituted milk powder or diluted evaporated milk; see page 15.

Wyoming Pan-Broiled Trout

Remove heads from fish if you need pan room, but leave tails on.

1/4 cup shortening, butter or margarine
6 to 8 whole trout
1 tablespoon lemon juice
Salt and pepper to taste
1 egg or equivalent
2 tablespoons evaporated milk
1-1/2 cups soft breadcrumbs

1/4 cup butter or margarine
2 tablespoons chopped canned mushroom
  stems and pieces
1/4 teaspoon seasoned salt
1/2 teaspoon dried leaf parsley
1 lemon, cut into wedges for garnish
2 teaspoons lemon juice

In a large skillet, melt 1/4 cup shortening, butter or margarine; set aside. Brush trout inside and outside with 1 tablespoon lemon juice. Sprinkle with salt and pepper. In a pie pan, beat egg and evaporated milk until blended. Pour breadcrumbs into another pie pan. Dip each trout into beaten egg mixture, then in breadcrumbs. Arrange crumb-coated fish in skillet. Pan-broil in melted fat over medium heat. Cook 3 to 5 minutes on each side until fish is lightly browned and flakes easily when pierced with a fork. Arrange cooked fish on a platter. Keep warm. In a small saucepan, melt 1/4 cup butter or margarine. Add mushrooms, seasoned salt and parsley; sauté 2 to 3 minutes. Arrange lemon wedges around trout. Stir 2 teaspoons lemon juice into sautéed mushroom mixture. Pour into a small bowl. Serve with trout. Makes 4 to 6 servings.

How to Make Wyoming Pan-Broiled Trout

1/Cook fish until it is lightly browned and flakes easily when pierced with a fork.

2/Cut lemon into wedges for garnish. Arrange lemon wedges around trout on platter.

Aspic Tuna Ring

Cut the aspic into 1-inch slices and serve it on crisp lettuce greens.

Aspic Ring, see below
3 tablespoons dried chopped
   mixed vegetables
6 tablespoons hot water
1 (11-oz.) can mandarin orange segments,
   drained
1 (4-oz.) can sliced water chestnuts,
   drained

1 (7-oz.) can chunk tuna
1 tablespoon chopped pimiento
1 tablespoon lemon juice
About 1/4 cup mayonnaise
1/4 teaspoon salt
Pinch of white pepper
Canned or cooked frozen French-cut
   green beans for garnish

Aspic Ring:
2 tablespoons unflavored gelatin powder
1/2 cup cold water
2-1/2 cups tomato juice
1/4 teaspoon onion salt

1/2 teaspoon salt
1/4 teaspoon celery salt
1 teaspoon sugar
1 tablespoon wine vinegar

Prepare Aspic Ring; refrigerate at least 4 hours before filling. Combine dried vegetables and hot water in a small bowl. Let stand 10 to 15 minutes to rehydrate vegetables. Combine rehydrated vegetables, mandarin orange segments, water chestnuts, tuna and pimiento in a medium bowl. Combine lemon juice, 2 tablespoons mayonnaise, salt and white pepper in a small bowl. Gently stir into tuna mixture. Invert chilled Aspic Ring onto a wet, round platter. Remove ring mold. Spoon tuna mixture into center of ring. Top with remaining mayonnaise. Garnish with French-cut beans. Makes about 6 servings.

Aspic Ring:
Wipe inside of a 7-inch, 1-quart ring mold with an oil-dampened paper towel; set aside. In a small bowl, sprinkle gelatin powder over cold water. Stir and let stand to soften. Combine remaining ingredients in a medium saucepan. Stir occasionally over medium heat until mixture simmers. Stir in gelatin mixture until completely dissolved. Pour into prepared ring mold and refrigerate 4 to 6 hours or overnight.

Butter-Flavor Topping

Spoon it over broiled fish, grilled meats, hot vegetables or noodles.

1 (1/2-oz.) pkg. butter-flavor granules
1/2 cup vegetable oil
1/8 teaspoon salt

Pinch of pepper
1 teaspoon Herb Seasoning, page 54

Combine all ingredients in a small jar with a tight-fitting lid. Cover and shake well. Makes about 1/2 cup.

Aspic Tuna Ring and Refrigerated Rolls, page 123

Mackerel Croquettes

Serve crisp and golden croquettes for a super fish dish.

Tartar Sauce, page 75, or Tangy
  Tomato Sauce, page 75
1 cup Savory Mushroom Sauce, below
1 (15-oz.) can jack mackerel
1 cup fine dry breadcrumbs

Pinch of salt
1 tablespoon lemon juice
Oil for deep-frying
Breadcrumbs for coating
1 egg, beaten, or equivalent

Prepare Tartar Sauce or Tangy Tomato Sauce. Prepare Savory Mushroom Sauce; cool. Turn mackerel into a large bowl. Drain liquid from mackerel; remove bones if desired. Discard liquid and bones. Use 2 forks to flake fish. Stir mushroom sauce, 1 cup breadcrumbs, salt and lemon juice into flaked mackerel. Pour oil 3 inches deep in a medium saucepan. Heat to 375F (190C). At this temperature a 1-inch cube of bread will turn golden brown in 50 seconds. Use your hands to shape fish mixture into balls about 1-1/2 inches in diameter. Roll fish balls in breadcrumbs to coat. Dip into beaten egg, then in breadcrumbs again. Use a slotted spoon to lower crumb-coated balls carefully into hot oil. Fry in hot oil until golden brown, turning as often as needed. Use slotted spoon to remove fried croquettes from hot oil. Drain on paper towels. Pour Tartar Sauce or Tangy Tomato Sauce into a serving bowl. Serve hot croquettes with sauce. Makes about 4 servings.

Savory Mushroom Sauce

A perfect sauce for any broiled or baked fish.

3/4 cup boiling water
1 chicken bouillon cube
1/4 cup butter or margarine
1 (4-oz.) can mushroom stems and pieces,
  drained
2 tablespoons all-purpose flour

3/4 cup evaporated milk
1/8 teaspoon paprika
1/2 teaspoon salt
1 teaspoon dried leaf parsley, crushed
1 teaspoon lemon juice

In a small bowl, pour boiling water over bouillon cube. Stir to dissolve. Melt butter or margarine in a large skillet or heavy saucepan. Add mushrooms; sauté over medium-low heat 2 to 3 minutes. Stir in flour until blended. Slowly stir in bouillon and evaporated milk. Cook and stir over medium-high heat until bubbly and slightly thickened. Stir in paprika, salt, parsley and lemon juice. Makes about 1-1/2 cups.

When beginning a long-term storage plan, one of the major problems you'll encounter is how to store the meat you expect to consume in the course of several months. Try setting a limit of red meat twice a week. Use chicken, fish and cheese for other main dishes.

Canned beef is very tasty—especially if it's used in casseroles and skillet dishes. It comes both with and without gravy. If you've never tried canned beef, start with Campers' Beef & Barley Stew or Juan Ramón's Chimichangas.

Canned ham is available in 2 forms: The larger cans are for baking and smaller cans of ground ham are ideal for spreads and salads. If you like ham, it's a good idea to store 2 to 4 large canned hams. Baked glazed ham is the answer when you have a houseful to feed for a special occasion; see Festive Ham. Read the labels carefully. Some canned hams require refrigeration. Cans of ground ham are wonderful for quick scrambled ham and eggs, sandwich spreads, salads and casseroles. Our version of the delicious southern dish, Hoppin' John, uses canned ground ham.

Frozen Meat

Buy fresh meat in large packages and divide it into smaller amounts needed for 1 meal. Whole, halved and quartered animals can be bought and cut up and packaged according to your needs. Consider the cost per pound, amount of waste bone and fat versus the cost of trimmed meat per pound at the market. Does the convenience of either outweigh the cost? How many pounds of meat does your family consume in a year?

To freeze meat, remove it from its packaging and cut off extra fat. Freeze the fat separately and use it to flavor beans and stews. Fat may become rancid if kept frozen for a long time so use it within a few months. Wrap meat securely in freezer wrap. If there are bones that could tear the wrapping, cover them with waxed paper or several thicknesses of freezer wrap. Place 2 pieces of freezer wrap or waxed paper between patties or chops so they will be easy to separate. If you have several small packages of the same kind of meat such as bacon, pork cubes or ground beef, drop them into 1 large freezer bag and tie the bag with a twist tie. You'll be able to locate small packages much faster if they're stored together.

Meat is best thawed in the refrigerator. Transfer it from the freezer to the refrigerator the day before you plan to use it. If you don't use it that day, it will still be good for use on the following day.

Beef and lamb can be frozen for 9 to 12 months. Pork can be frozen up to 6 months. Use organ meats, ground meats and meat cubes within 3 to 4 months.

Meat

International Gathering

Sweet & Sour Chicken Wings, page 33
West African Beef Stew, page 86
Split Peas Punjabi-Style, page 65
French Bread, page 126
Strawberry-Rhubarb Cream, page 110

Savory Pot Roast

When unexpected guests appear, raid your pantry for dried vegetables.

1/3 cup all-purpose flour
1/2 teaspoon salt
1/2 teaspoon pepper
1 (3- to 4-lb.) chuck roast
1 tablespoon bacon drippings or
   vegetable oil
2 cups boiling water
1 beef bouillon cube
1/2 cup red wine or 1/4 cup wine vinegar

2 tablespoons dried chopped onion
2 tablespoons dried chopped celery
1 tablespoon dried leaf parsley
2 tablespoons dried shredded carrots
2 tablespoons mixed dried chopped peppers
1/2 teaspoon garlic powder
1/2 teaspoon ground marjoram
1/2 teaspoon ground thyme
About 3 tablespoons water

On waxed paper, mix flour, salt and pepper. Coat meat with flour mixture. Reserve excess flour mixture for gravy. Melt drippings or heat oil in a large heavy pot or Dutch oven over medium-high heat. Brown meat on both sides in drippings or oil. Remove pot from heat. In a medium bowl, pour boiling water over bouillon cube. Stir to dissolve. Add remaining ingredients except 3 tablespoons water. Pour bouillon mixture over meat. Add more water to cover, if necessary. Bring to a boil; reduce heat. Cover and simmer until meat is tender, 2-1/2 to 3 hours. Remove from heat. Place meat on a platter, leaving gravy in pot. Keep meat warm. In a small bowl, stir 3 tablespoons water into reserved flour mixture to make a paste. Stir about 1/3 cup gravy into paste. Stir flour mixture into gravy in pot. Cook over medium heat about 10 minutes. Ladle a little gravy over meat. Serve remaining gravy separately. Makes 8 servings.

Beef & Barley Stew

A substantial stew for a cold evening.

1 (16-oz.) can mixed vegetables
Water
2 tablespoons mixed dried chopped peppers
1 tablespoon dried minced onion
1 tablespoon dried chopped celery
1/2 cup pearl barley
1/2 teaspoon dried leaf marjoram

1/8 teaspoon black pepper
1 bay leaf
1/8 teaspoon garlic powder
1 (8-oz.) can tomato sauce
1 beef bouillon cube
1 (12-oz.) can roast beef with gravy

Drain vegetables, reserving liquid. Add water to reserved liquid to make 3 cups. In a large saucepan, combine liquid, peppers, onion, celery, barley, marjoram, black pepper, bay leaf, garlic powder, tomato sauce and bouillon cube. Bring to a boil; reduce heat. Cover and simmer 50 minutes. Add vegetables and beef. Bring to a boil; reduce heat. Cover and simmer 10 minutes. Remove bay leaf. Serve hot. Makes 6 servings.

Variations

Substitute 1/2 pound cooked crumbled ground beef for the canned beef.

Camper's Beef & Barley Stew: In a food-storage bag, combine peppers, onion, celery, barley, marjoram, black pepper, bay leaf, garlic powder and bouillon cube. Store with canned mixed vegetables, canned tomato sauce, canned roast beef and a measuring cup. Cook as directed.

Van Horne Meat Loaves

Individual meat loaves in decorated pastry can be frozen and baked later.

1 lb. ground beef
1 lb. ground pork
1/2 cup fine breadcrumbs
1/2 cup tomato juice
2 tablespoons dried minced onion
2 tablespoons instant milk powder
2 tablespoons Worcestershire sauce
2 tablespoons cider vinegar

1 teaspoon salt
1 teaspoon chili powder
1/2 teaspoon pepper
1/2 teaspoon dried leaf basil, crushed
Flaky Pie Pastry or Rich Pie Pastry for
   double-crust pie, page 113
Savory Mushroom Sauce, page 80
About 3 teaspoons milk

Preheat oven to 375F (190C). Mix all ingredients except pastry and sauce in a large bowl. Divide mixture equally into five 5-1/2" x 3" loaf pans, packing loosely and smoothing surface of each loaf. Bake 35 minutes. Remove from oven. Pour off grease from each loaf. Loosen each loaf with a metal spatula, if necessary. Turn out onto wire racks over baking sheets. Cool completely. When loaves are cooled, prepare pastry dough. Divide dough into 5 equal portions. Roll out each portion to an 8-inch square. Place 1 meat loaf in the center of each square. Cut out a small square from each corner so ends and sides will fold up neatly. Fold ends up; moisten with water. Fold up sides; press to seal. Cut designs from dough trimmings. Use water to attach dough cutouts to loaves. Wrap each loaf in freezer wrap and freeze. To prepare frozen meat loaves, thaw in refrigerator 3 to 5 hours. Preheat oven to 375F (190C). Lightly grease a baking sheet. Unwrap meat loaves. Brush tops and sides with milk. Place on prepared baking sheet. Bake about 30 minutes until golden. Prepare Savory Mushroom Sauce. To serve, spoon sauce over meat loaves. Makes 5 individual meat loaves.

How to Make Van Horne Meat Loaves

1/Place a meat loaf on a dough square. Cut small squares from corners of dough. Fold up ends and sides.

2/Cut designs from dough trimmings and attach to loaves.

Beef Sate

You'll need skewers and hot coals for this Indonesian barbecue.

1-1/2 lbs. beef stew-meat, partially frozen	1/2 teaspoon garlic powder
1/4 cup soy sauce	1/4 teaspoon ground ginger
1 tablespoon unsulfured molasses	1/4 teaspoon ground cumin
2 tablespoons lime juice or lemon juice	1/8 teaspoon red (cayenne) pepper
	Peanut Butter Sauce, see below

Peanut Butter Sauce:

1/4 cup peanut butter	1/2 teaspoon ground ginger
2 tablespoons soy sauce	1/2 teaspoon garlic powder
2 tablespoons brown sugar	1 teaspoon ground coriander
1 tablespoon lime juice or lemon juice	1/2 cup milk

Cut beef into 1-inch cubes. Put in a plastic bag and place bag in a baking pan. In a small bowl, combine soy sauce, molasses, lime or lemon juice, garlic powder, ginger, cumin and red pepper. Pour over beef in plastic bag. Secure with a twist tie. Turn bag to mix well. Refrigerate bag in baking pan 8 to 24 hours, turning bag occasionally to mix meat and marinade. About 1 hour before serving, prepare Peanut Butter Sauce. Place over low heat while cooking meat; stir occasionally. Thread meat on skewers. Cook on grill 5 to 10 minutes until tender, turning frequently and basting with marinade. Serve with warm Peanut Butter Sauce. Makes 6 to 8 servings.

Peanut Butter Sauce:
Combine peanut butter, soy sauce, brown sugar, lime or lemon juice, ginger, garlic powder and coriander in a small saucepan; mix to blend. Gradually stir in milk. Keep sauce warm.

Orange Grove Pork Chops

A delightful dish to serve with rice or noodles.

3 lbs. pork chops	1/8 teaspoon garlic powder
About 2 tablespoons vegetable oil	2 teaspoons grated orange peel
1 cup boiling water	1/8 teaspoon ground thyme
1 chicken bouillon cube	1/2 cup water, if needed
2 tablespoons dried chopped onion	1 orange, sliced
1/2 teaspoon sugar	

Trim excess fat from pork chops. Heat oil in a large skillet. Add pork chops and brown on both sides over medium-high heat. Remove chops as they brown, adding more oil if needed. When all chops are browned, remove skillet from heat. In a small bowl, pour boiling water over bouillon cube. Stir to dissolve. Pour into skillet. Return skillet to heat. Stir in remaining ingredients except orange slices. Add browned pork chops. Cover and simmer 40 minutes, turning and rearranging chops in skillet halfway through cooking time. Add more water, if needed. To serve, arrange orange slices around the edge of a platter. Place pork chops in the center. Spoon sauce from skillet over chops. Makes 8 to 10 servings.

Juan Ramón's Chimichangas

A Southwestern specialty.

2 medium potatoes, unpeeled
2 large onions
1/2 cup vegetable oil
1 tablespoon dried leaf oregano
1/4 teaspoon paprika
1/4 teaspoon garlic powder
1/4 teaspoon pepper
2 (4-oz.) cans chopped green chilies
2 (16-oz.) cans tomatoes, chopped,
   drained, juice reserved

1/2 teaspoon salt
1/4 teaspoon chili powder
2 (12-oz.) cans roast beef with gravy
4 cups shredded Longhorn cheese (1 lb.)
24 (8-inch) flour tortillas
About 1 cup vegetable oil
Carroll's Salsa, page 68, or other salsa

Wash potatoes and dice into 1/4- to 1/2-inch cubes. Dice onions. Heat a large heavy skillet or Dutch oven over medium heat. Heat 1/2 cup oil in hot skillet about 2 minutes. Add diced potatoes, diced onions, oregano, paprika, garlic powder and pepper. Cook over medium-low heat, stirring frequently. When onions are tender, stir in green chilies, tomatoes, 1 cup reserved liquid from tomatoes, salt and chili powder. Break up roast beef with a fork. Stir into vegetable mixture with gravy. Cover and cook until potatoes are tender, stirring frequently. Let cool to room temperature. Refrigerate until ready to make chimichangas. To assemble each chimichanga, place about 2 tablespoons cheese in the middle of a tortilla; spoon about 3 tablespoons meat and vegetable mixture on top of cheese; fold over each side and both ends of tortilla to make a closed packet. Heat about 1 cup oil in a wok or large heavy skillet to 375F (190C). At this temperature, a 1-inch cube of bread will turn golden brown in about 50 seconds. Fry chimichangas two or three at a time until golden brown, about 3 minutes. Turn once during frying. Drain on paper towels. To serve, top each chimichanga with Carroll's Salsa. To freeze extra chimichangas, wrap each one in freezer wrap and place in a freezer bag; secure with a twist tie and store in freezer. Unwrap thawed frozen chimichangas and heat in broiler 2 to 5 minutes. Makes 24 chimichangas.

Freeze whole oranges, lemons and limes for garnishing; see page 11.

West African Beef Stew

Pineapple slices and spicy chutney enhance this exotic dish.

1/4 cup dried chopped onion
1 cup tomato juice
1 cup boiling water
1 beef bouillon cube
2 lbs. beef stew-meat, partially frozen
2 tablespoons vegetable oil
1 (8-oz.) can tomato sauce
1/2 teaspoon curry powder
1/2 teaspoon ground ginger
6 drops hot pepper sauce

1/2 teaspoon salt
1 tablespoon vegetable oil
1 garlic clove, halved
1 cup uncooked long-grain rice
2 cups water or vegetable stock
1/2 teaspoon salt
1 (8-oz.) can pineapple slices
Mixed Fruit Chutney, page 145, or
    other chutney
1 cup cocktail peanuts

Combine onion and tomato juice in a small bowl. Let stand 10 to 15 minutes to rehydrate onion. In a small bowl, pour boiling water over bouillon cube. Stir to dissolve; set aside. Cut beef into 1-1/2-inch cubes. Heat 2 tablespoons oil over medium heat in a large pot. Add stew-meat. Brown on all sides, removing each piece as it is browned. Remove pot from heat. Return all meat to pot. Add bouillon, tomato sauce and tomato juice with rehydrated onion. Stir in curry powder, ginger, hot pepper sauce and salt. Bring to a boil; reduce heat. Cover and simmer until meat is tender, about 2 hours. About 30 minutes before serving, heat 1 tablespoon oil in a medium saucepan with a tight-fitting lid over low heat. Add garlic halves. Cook, turning garlic frequently until golden; do not burn. Remove garlic. Add rice to garlic oil; stir to coat with oil. Stir frequently over medium-high heat until rice is golden. Remove saucepan from heat. Let cool slightly. Pour in water or vegetable stock. Add salt. Return to medium heat and bring to a boil. Reduce heat to low. Cover and cook about 20 minutes until liquid is absorbed and rice is tender. Keep warm until ready to serve. Cut each pineapple slice in half. Mound stew over hot rice on each plate. Serve chutney, peanuts and pineapple in small bowls or on a relish tray. Makes 4 to 6 servings.

Variation
Omit the rice and serve the beef mixture in warmed pita bread halves.

Ginger

Recipes in this book call for ground ginger. Fresh ginger can be peeled and stored in a container of dry sherry or white vinegar. Slice the ginger or leave it whole. Put it in a small container with a tight-fitting lid. Add enough sherry or vinegar to cover the ginger. Cover tightly. Fresh ginger can be refrigerated for several months. Ginger may absorb enough vinegar flavor to be obvious in sweet dishes. If you plan to use it for desserts, store it in sherry.

Unpeeled ginger can be frozen for several months. Wrap it well. Cut off pieces as you need them.

In general, 1 teaspoon of minced fresh ginger equals 1/2 teaspoon ground ginger.

West African Beef Stew and Mixed Fruit Chutney, page 145

Treasure House Beef Mix

You will be able to get several varied dishes out of this batch of Mix.

3/4 to 1 cup dried chopped onion
1 teaspoon dried minced garlic
1/2 cup dried leaf parsley or
   celery leaves
1 cup water
5 lbs. lean ground beef
1 tablespoon salt
Pepper to taste

1/4 cup Worcestershire sauce
1/2 teaspoon celery salt
2 (16-oz.) cans tomato sauce
1/2 teaspoon ground thyme
1 teaspoon dried leaf oregano
1/2 teaspoon ground cumin
1 teaspoon ground marjoram

In a small bowl, combine onion, garlic, parsley or celery leaves and water. Let stand 15 minutes. Brown beef in a large pot or Dutch oven, stirring with a fork to crumble. Stir in onion mixture, salt, pepper, Worcestershire sauce, celery salt, tomato sauce, thyme, oregano, cumin and marjoram. Spoon off fat as it rises to the surface. Cook about 30 minutes until flavors blend, stirring occasionally. Cool. Spoon into seven 2-cup containers with tight-fitting lids. Store in refrigerator up to 7 days or in freezer up to 4 months. Use to prepare the following dishes. Makes about 14 cups.

Use Treasure House Beef Mix to make:

Speedy Stroganoff: Thaw and heat 1 package (2 cups) beef mixture. Stir in 1 (4-oz.) can mushroom stems and pieces and 1 (10-1/2-oz.) can condensed cream of mushroom soup. Simmer over medium heat until bubbly, about 5 minutes. Spoon over egg noodles, rice or whole-wheat kernels. Makes 4 servings.

Deep-Dish Pizza: Thaw and heat 1 package (2 cups) beef mixture. Prepare pizza dough from Hearty Pizza, page 90. Press dough over bottom and up sides of a lightly greased 13" x 9" baking pan. Spread 1/2 cup tomato sauce evenly over bottom of dough. Pour hot meat mixture over crust. Sprinkle with 2 cups shredded mozzarella or Cheddar cheese. Bake 20 to 25 minutes in 425F (220C) oven. Makes 4 to 6 servings.

Treasure House Casserole: Thaw and heat 1 package (2 cups) beef mixture in a stovetop casserole. Cook and mash 4 potatoes. Stir in 1/2 cup evaporated milk and 1/4 cup butter or margarine until smooth. Or prepare instant mashed potatoes to make 4 servings, omitting salt. Spoon prepared potatoes over hot meat mixture. Top with 1/4 to 1/2 cup finely shredded Longhorn or Monterey Jack cheese. Bake 20 to 25 minutes in 375F (190C) oven until cheese melts and mixture bubbles. Makes 4 to 6 servings.

Quick Baked Chimichangas: Thaw and heat 1 package (2 cups) beef mixture. Stir in 1 cup drained canned whole-kernel corn. Thaw twelve 8-inch flour tortillas. Heat each briefly on an ungreased griddle. Spoon about 1/4 cup meat mixture onto center of each tortilla. Fold 1 end of tortilla over mixture then fold 2 sides over. Roll up and place on a baking sheet. Brush each with melted butter or margarine. Bake in 350F (175C) oven about 20 minutes until lightly browned. Makes 6 to 8 servings.

Treasure House Roll-Ups: Thaw and heat 1 package (2 cups) beef mixture. Spoon off as much liquid as possible. Prepare pizza dough from Hearty Pizza, page 90. Roll out to a 15" x 12" rectangle 1/4 inch thick. Leaving a 1/2-inch strip uncovered along 1 long side of rectangle, spread 1 cup beef mix evenly over dough. Roll up lengthwise, starting from long side that is covered with beef. Pinch to seal. Use a sharp knife to cut in 1-1/2-inch slices. Spread remaining beef mixture evenly in a 13" x 9" baking pan. Arrange roll-ups cut-side up over beef mixture. Bake in 350F (175C) oven 20 to 25 minutes until dough is golden brown. Makes 5 or 6 servings.

How to Use Treasure House Beef Mix to Make Deep-Dish Pizza

1/Press dough over bottom and up sides of baking pan.

2/Spread tomato sauce and meat mixture over dough. Sprinkle with cheese.

Barbecued Luncheon Meat

Luncheon meat is dressed up with a spicy sauce.

1 (16-oz.) can sliced cling peaches
1 (8-oz.) can tomato sauce
1/4 cup packed brown sugar
3 tablespoons cider vinegar
1/2 teaspoon salt

1/2 teaspoon Worcestershire sauce
1 teaspoon dry mustard
1-1/2 teaspoons dried chopped onion
1/2 teaspoon chili powder
1 (12-oz.) can luncheon meat

Drain peaches, reserving juice for another purpose. Reserve 8 peach slices; cut remaining slices into 2 or 3 pieces. In a large saucepan or skillet, combine peach pieces, tomato sauce, brown sugar, vinegar, salt, Worcestershire sauce, dry mustard, onion and chili powder. Bring to a boil over medium-high heat. Simmer over low heat, about 5 minutes. Drain drippings from luncheon meat. Place meat on a cutting board. Without cutting all the way through bottom, make 8 cuts in meat, making 9 slices. Insert 1 reserved peach slice into each cut in meat. Place sliced meat and peaches in sauce. Cover saucepan or skillet; simmer until meat is hot, about 15 minutes. To serve, place luncheon meat on a small platter. Spoon about 1/2 cup sauce over meat. Pour remaining sauce into a small serving bowl. Makes 4 or 5 servings.

Shockey Farm Pork Pot

Delicious served over noodles.

1 tablespoon vegetable oil
1 (3- to 4-lb.) pork loin, trimmed
1 large onion, cut in wedges
1 (16-oz.) can tomatoes, chopped
1 bay leaf
1/2 teaspoon dried leaf basil, crushed
1/2 teaspoon ground coriander

1/2 teaspoon pepper
1/2 teaspoon salt
1 tablespoon dried chopped celery
1/3 cup red wine vinegar
1 (10-oz.) can whole baby clams
1 teaspoon cornstarch
2 teaspoons water

In a large heavy pot or Dutch oven, heat oil over medium-high heat. Brown pork on all sides. Remove from pot; set aside. Reduce heat to low. Add onion to pot. Stir and cook until onion is golden. Add tomatoes, bay leaf, basil, coriander, pepper, salt and celery. Place browned pork on top of vegetable mixture. Pour vinegar over pork. Cover and cook over low heat about 3 hours until meat is tender. Strain clam juice. Add juice to pork. Rinse clams in a bowl of cold water to remove any shells. Add rinsed clams to pork. Simmer 10 minutes. Remove pot from heat. Remove pork and slice. In a small bowl, dissolve cornstarch in water to make a paste. Spoon a little cooking liquid from pork into cornstarch paste; mix well. Add to cooking liquid in pot. Stir over medium-low heat until thickened. Serve hot gravy over sliced pork. Makes 6 to 8 servings.

Hearty Pizza

Yeast makes the dough easy to handle and fast to rise.

Pizza Sauce, see below
1 envelope active dry yeast
   (1 tablespoon)
About 3/4 cup warm water or milk
2-1/2 cups Basic Baking Mix, page 121

1-1/2 cups shredded mozzarella cheese
   (6 oz.)
1-1/2 cups cooked crumbled sausage or
   ground beef
1 teaspoon dried leaf oregano, crushed

Pizza Sauce:
1 tablespoon dried chopped onion
1 tablespoon hot water
1 (8-oz.) can tomato sauce
1/2 teaspoon salt

Pepper to taste
Pinch of ground cumin
Pinch of ground marjoram
1 teaspoon Worcestershire sauce

Preheat oven to 400F (205C). Prepare Pizza Sauce; set aside. Add yeast to water or milk. Let stand until foamy. In a medium bowl, stir yeast mixture into Basic Baking Mix. Turn out onto a lightly floured board. Knead about 15 times. Divide dough in half. Roll out each half to a 12-inch circle, 1/8 inch thick. Place each circle in a 12-inch pizza pan. Spread sauce evenly over each circle. Top each with half the cheese and half the cooked meat. Sprinkle evenly with oregano. Bake 15 to 20 minutes until dough browns. Makes two 12-inch pizzas or 8 to 12 servings.

Pizza Sauce:
Combine onion and hot water in a small bowl. Let stand 10 to 15 minutes to rehydrate onion. Stir in remaining ingredients.

Corn Bread Pie

Corn bread tops a succulent corn-and-beef mixture.

1 cup hot water
3 tablespoons dried chopped onion
1 tablespoon butter or margarine
1 lb. ground beef
1 (8-oz.) can tomato sauce
1/4 teaspoon ground cumin
1/8 teaspoon ground marjoram
1/4 teaspoon celery salt
1/2 teaspoon salt

1/4 teaspoon pepper
1 teaspoon chili powder
About 1/3 cup water
1 (12-oz.) can whole-kernel corn, undrained
2 tablespoons dried chopped mixed vegetables
Cornmeal Topper, see below
1/2 teaspoon dried leaf parsley

Cornmeal Topper:
3/4 cup cornmeal
1 tablespoon sugar
1 tablespoon all-purpose flour
1-1/2 teaspoons baking powder
1/4 teaspoon salt

1 egg, beaten, or equivalent
1/2 cup milk
1 tablespoon bacon drippings or vegetable oil

Butter a 2-quart casserole; set aside. Combine hot water and onion in a small bowl. Let stand 10 to 15 minutes to rehydrate onion. Melt butter or margarine in a medium skillet over medium heat. Drain rehydrated onion, reserving liquid. Sauté onion in melted butter or margarine until browned. Add ground beef, breaking it up with a fork. Cook until lightly browned. Stir in tomato sauce, cumin, marjoram, celery salt, salt, pepper and chili powder. Add water to reserved onion water to make 1 cup. Stir into meat mixture. Simmer 15 minutes to blend flavors. Preheat oven to 350F (175C). Stir corn with liquid and dried mixed vegetables into meat mixture. Simmer until heated through, about 5 minutes. Prepare Cornmeal Topper. Pour meat mixture into prepared casserole. Pour Cornmeal Topper over meat mixture. Bake 20 to 25 minutes until Cornmeal Topper rises and becomes crisp on top. Sprinkle with parsley. Makes 6 servings.

Cornmeal Topper:
Thoroughly combine cornmeal, sugar, flour, baking powder and salt in a medium bowl. Stir egg, milk and bacon drippings or vegetable oil together. Add to cornmeal mixture. Stir until all ingredients are moistened.

Common Sense

We do not recommend that you live on stored foods all year round. It is a good idea to combine fresh, frozen, canned and dried foods in your daily meal planning. For example, if you make a fresh spinach salad, toss in some cooked frozen peas, or use dried onion and dried leaf parsley in the dressing. Making coleslaw? Fresh cabbage and canned corn go well together. Use fresh eggs with canned vegetables for a quiche. Adding reconstituted instant milk powder to fresh milk is economical and nutritious.

Catalina Rolled Steak

You'll need a 5-hour head start to prepare this.

1 (1-1/2-lb.) piece beef flank steak or
  boneless round steak
1/2 teaspoon whole allspice
1/3 cup wine vinegar or red wine
2 tablespoons olive oil
1/4 teaspoon garlic powder
1/2 cup fine dry breadcrumbs
1 tablespoon mixed dried chopped peppers
1 tablespoon dried minced onion
1/2 teaspoon celery salt

1 teaspoon ground majoram
1/8 teaspoon black pepper
1 (4-oz.) can mushroom stems and pieces
2 tablespoons all-purpose flour
1/2 teaspoon salt
1/8 teaspoon black pepper
1 to 2 tablespoons vegetable oil or
  bacon drippings
1 cup water

Unroll steak on a flat surface. Pound with a mallet or the blunt edge of a heavy knife to tenderize the steak. Place in a large baking pan or on a large platter. Combine allspice, vinegar or wine, olive oil and garlic powder in a small bowl. Pour over steak. Marinate at room temperature 3 to 4 hours, turning occasionally. Combine breadcrumbs, peppers, onion, celery salt, majoram and 1/8 teaspoon black pepper. Drain mushrooms, reserving liquid. In a blender or food processor, finely chop mushrooms with 3 tablespoons reserved liquid. Add to breadcrumb mixture; mix well. Drain steak, reserving marinade. Spread mushroom mixture down center of steak following the grain. Roll up starting from a long side. Tie with kitchen twine in middle, at each end and across lengthwise. Mix flour, salt and 1/8 teaspoon pepper in a plate. Coat rolled steak with flour mixture. Heat a large deep skillet or Dutch oven over medium heat. Add vegetable oil or bacon drippings. Brown rolled steak in hot oil or drippings. Remove from heat. Pour water over steak; add reserved marinade. Bring to a boil over medium heat. Reduce heat. Cover and simmer about 1 hour until meat is tender. Place steak on a platter; remove twine. Remove whole allspice from gravy. Slice steak. Serve gravy separately. Makes 6 servings.

How to Make Catalina Rolled Steak

1/Spread mushroom mixture down the center of steak. Roll up from a long side.

2/Tie up rolled steak securely.

Poor-Boy Casserole

Vary this oven meal by baking the biscuits on top of the casserole.

1 lb. lean ground beef	**1 (8-oz.) can tomato sauce**
2 tablespoons mixed dried chopped peppers	**1/4 teaspoon ground marjoram**
1/4 cup hot water	**1/8 teaspoon celery salt**
1/2 cup chopped fresh onion	**1/8 teaspoon ground cumin**
1 (29-oz.) can pork and beans	**Country Biscuits, page 121**

Preheat oven to 350F (175C). In a 2-quart casserole, break beef into small pieces. Place in pre-heating oven 15 minutes until lightly browned, stirring once. Combine peppers and hot water in a small bowl. Let stand 10 to 15 minutes to rehydrate peppers. Stir rehydrated peppers and onion into meat mixture. Return to oven; bake 10 minutes. Stir in pork and beans, tomato sauce, marjoram, celery salt and cumin. Turn oven heat to 425F (220C). Return casserole to oven until hot, about 20 minutes. Bake Country Biscuits on a small baking sheet at the same time, removing from oven after about 12 minutes. Serve meat mixture over baked biscuits. Makes about 6 servings.

he recipes in this section are easy to use and the foods are all nutritious. Become accustomed to the flavor and texture of whole-wheat products by adding a few cooked whole kernels of wheat to casseroles. Grind some of the cooked kernels and add them to ground meat dishes.

Wheat is the first choice when you consider storing grains. It is easy to store and has high nutritive value. It is especially rich in protein, iron, calcium, niacin, thiamin and riboflavin. When sprouted, page 96, it also supplies vitamins A and C. For information on storing other grains, see page 14.

Choose storage wheat carefully. Select Grade 1, low-moisture wheat such as dark Turkey red Winter wheat, dark hard Spring wheat or Marquis wheat.

Store wheat properly. Hard, dry wheat stores best. Use airtight metal containers that will keep insects, rodents and moisture out. Plastic containers with airtight seals can also be used, but are more easily cracked or broken. The best container for wheat storage is a metal, airtight, 5-gallon can with a 2-1/2- to 7-inch lid. Three 5-gallon cans will hold about 100 pounds of wheat. They can be stacked to save space. Store wheat in a dry, dark place where the temperature is between 45F and 70F (5C and 20C). If you live in a warm climate where underground storage stays above 70F (20C), keep your wheat as dry as possible. Place 2" x 4" boards under all containers to raise them off cement floors. Leave an airspace between cement walls and storage containers. This prevents collection of moisture. Properly stored wheat can be preserved 10 years or longer without losing nutritional value.

Protect your wheat. Use one of the following fumigation methods to protect your wheat from an infestation:

● Spread 4 ounces of crushed dry ice over the bottom of a 5-gallon metal can. Or place a 1-inch layer of wheat in a plastic container, then layer dry ice over it. Fill the container with wheat. Set the lid ajar, allowing dry-ice fumes to escape. After 30 minutes cover the can tightly. Watch the can for 3 to 4 minutes. If it bulges, carefully remove the lid to let fumes escape. Leave the lid off about 2 minutes, then replace it.

● Pour wheat into plastic food bags. Tie the tops securely. Store in the freezer 4 or 5 days at 0F (−20C). If you have a large amount of wheat, take it to a commercial frozen-food storage plant. As the bags are removed from the freezer, place them in metal or heavy plastic canisters. Remove and use the bags of wheat one at a time. This process should be repeated in about 30 days to kill any eggs that may have hatched.

● Pour wheat 1/2 inch deep in a shallow baking pan. Place for 20 minutes **but no longer** in a 150F (65C) oven. There is a danger of scorching wheat in the oven, so follow directions carefully. If necessary, open the oven door slightly to prevent overheating and to let moisture escape. Thorough heating destroys all stages of insect pests.

If your wheat is badly infested and insects have burrowed into the wheat kernel, you may not be able to save it for home use. It can be fed to farm animals.

Moisture content in wheat should be no more than 12%. Above this amount, fungus, bacteria and insects may begin to multiply. To test for moisture content, carefully weigh 20 ounces of wheat. Spread it over the bottom of a 13" x 9" baking pan. Bake 2 hours at 180F (80C). Weigh the wheat again. If the baked wheat has lost no more than 2 ounces, the moisture content is at a safe level. If more than 2 ounces was lost, moisture content is too high.

To reduce moisture, pour wheat 3/4 inch deep in shallow pans or trays. Heat 20 minutes in a 150F (65C) oven. Open the oven door slightly to let moisture escape.

Grind your own wheat. Whole-wheat kernels take up less space than flour and keep almost indefinitely. Whole-wheat flour can be stored only up to 6 months in a cool, dry place. If kept longer, it may develop a stale, rancid flavor.

The most convenient way to grind your wheat is with a *wheat grinder* or *grain mill.* You can grind wheat into flour or crack it for cereal using either piece of equipment.

Hand-powered wheat grinders or mills are inexpensive and do an adequate job. Electric grinders are expensive but save time and effort.

Look for ease in cleaning as you shop for a grinder. Some have enclosed cabinets or chambers that are next to impossible to clean. Surfaces where the flour is collected or where it passes through the grain mill should be smooth so flour doesn't build up in crevices. Collection pans or bags should be washable. Vacuum your grinder with the long thin nozzle of your vacuum cleaner at least once a week to remove sediment.

Motors on grinders should have proper shielding to protect the operator. Check the size and power of the motor. A grinder must be capable of continuously grinding at least 10 pounds of hard red Winter wheat into flour without the frame exceeding 142F (60C). It should be able to grind at least 50 pounds an hour. You should be able to start and stop the motor while in the process of grinding wheat. Grinders that convert from electric to hand or bicycle power are invaluable if there is a power outage.

Some communities have a local miller or health-food store willing to grind your wheat for you.

Introduce whole-wheat foods to your family a little at a time. Make the Whole-Wheat Blender Pancakes next weekend for an outstanding treat.

After you've made Polka-Dot Bread, treat your family to Nina's Whole-Grain Patties. They'll remind you of potato patties. Whole-wheat casseroles such as Wheat & Sausage Deep-Dish are much more chewy than similar hamburger casseroles. For a less dense and less chewy version, use the variation.

New-Neighbors Supper

Turkey Pilaf, page 101
Aspic Tuna Ring, page 78
Dinner Casserole Loaf, page 124
Whole-Wheat Refrigerator Cookies, page 149
Grandma's Secret Ice Cream, page 117

Wheat Sloppy Joes

A great supper for busy family members.

1/4 cup dried chopped onion
1/4 cup mixed dried chopped peppers
2 tablespoons dried chopped celery
About 1-1/4 cups hot water
1 lb. lean ground beef
1 (8-oz.) can tomato paste
1 (8-oz.) can tomato sauce

1/4 cup ketchup
Dash of hot pepper sauce
1/4 teaspoon chili powder
1 teaspoon cider vinegar
1/2 to 1 cup sprouted wheat, page 96
Salt and pepper to taste
4 to 6 hamburger buns

Combine onion, peppers, celery and 1 cup hot water in a medium bowl. Let stand 10 to 15 minutes to rehydrate vegetables. Add remaining 1/4 cup water if needed. In a large skillet, brown ground beef. Stir in rehydrated vegetables. Stir over medium low heat until tender but not browned, 2 minutes. Stir in remaining ingredients. Cover and simmer 15 minutes. Spoon over hamburger buns. Makes 4 to 6 servings.

Thermos Wheat

Combine wheat and hot water in a thermos tonight for tomorrow's cereal.

2 cups water   **1/2 teaspoon salt**
1 cup whole-wheat kernels

In a small saucepan, bring water to a boil. Pour about 1/2 cup boiling water into a 2-cup thermos. Cover and set aside. In a sieve, wash wheat under running water. Pour hot water from thermos. Spoon washed wheat into hot thermos. Add salt and remaining boiling water to about 1 inch from top of thermos. Attach lid. Let stand 6 hours or overnight. Serve cooked wheat with fruit as cereal or use in other recipes. Makes about 2 cups.

Slow-Cooked Wheat

A good method for preparing larger quantities of wheat.

3 cups whole-wheat kernels   **About 8 cups water**
1 teaspoon salt

In a large sieve, wash wheat under running water. Pour washed wheat into a slow cooker. Add salt and water. Cook on low heat 8 hours or overnight. Store in refrigerator in a non-metal container with a tight-fitting lid. Use within 3 weeks. Serve as cereal or use in other recipes. Makes about 8 cups.

How to Sprout Wheat

When sprouting wheat, select good quality, undamaged seeds. Discard any that are split, chipped or blemished. They tend to mold rather than sprout.

Bottle Sprouting Method:

Wash 3/4 cup wheat. Pour washed wheat into a quart jar. Cover with about 3/4 cup warm water. Set aside to soak 12 hours. Drain, reserving water to use in soup or a sauce. Rinse soaked wheat. Return rinsed wheat to jar. To keep insects out, cover mouth of jar with a clean piece of nylon stocking or cheesecloth. Hold in place with an elastic band. Lay jar on its side in a dark, warm cupboard. As wheat dries, sprinkle with a small amount of water 2 or 3 times a day.

Shallow-Dish Sprouting Method:

Cover the bottom of a shallow baking dish with a 1/4-inch layer of whole-wheat kernels that have been soaked as in bottle method. Fold a damp bath towel to fit dish and lay over wheat. Keep towel damp, but don't let wheat stand in water.

How to Make Thermos Wheat

1/Spoon wheat into hot thermos.

2/Serve cooked wheat with fruit as cereal.

Bulghur

Cracked dried cooked wheat, or bulghur, rehydrates and cooks quickly when added to casseroles.

**2 cups Slow-Cooked Wheat, opposite, or
  Thermos Wheat, opposite**

Prepare cooked wheat. Preheat oven to 150F (65C). Spread wheat in a 13" x 9" baking pan. Bake 2 hours or longer with oven door ajar until wheat is dried. Process dried cooked wheat in a blender or food processor until wheat is cracked. When added to casseroles or dishes having excess moisture, 1/2 cup bulghur will absorb 1/2 cup liquid. Bulghur can also be boiled 5 to 10 minutes with an equal amount of water. Bulghur doubles in volume when rehydrated with an equal amount of water. Makes about 1 cup.

Hamburger & Wheat Casserole

Prepare this dish early in the day and reheat it before serving.

1 lb. lean ground beef	1/4 teaspoon ground marjoram
1/2 cup hot water	1/4 teaspoon black pepper
2 tablespoons dried chopped onion	1/2 to 1 teaspoon poultry seasoning
1 tablespoon dried chopped green peppers	3/4 cup uncooked cracked wheat or
2 tablespoons dried chopped	3/4 cup bulghur, page 97
mixed vegetables	2 cups boiling water
1 teaspoon salt	1 cup tomato juice
1/4 teaspoon ground cumin	1 (8-oz.) can tomato sauce

In a large skillet, lightly brown ground beef. Add 1/2 cup hot water, onion, peppers, vegetable flakes, salt, cumin, marjoram, black pepper and poultry seasoning. Simmer over medium heat 5 minutes. Preheat oven to 325F (165C). In a 3-quart casserole, combine meat mixture, cracked wheat or bulghur, 2 cups boiling water, tomato juice and tomato sauce. Bake uncovered about 1-1/2 hours until cracked wheat or bulghur is tender. If casserole has absorbed most of liquid after 1 hour, cover for final 30 minutes. Makes about 6 servings.

Whole-Wheat Blender Pancakes

Small packages of whole-wheat kernels or berries can be purchased at health-food stores.

1 cup milk	1/4 cup vegetable oil
1 cup whole-wheat kernels	1/2 teaspoon salt
2 eggs, beaten, or equivalent	1 teaspoon baking soda
2 tablespoons sugar	2 teaspoons baking powder

Combine milk and whole-wheat kernels in a blender. Blend on high speed 3 to 4 minutes until wheat kernels are ground fine. Preheat griddle to 375F (190C) over medium heat. Reduce blender speed to medium. Add eggs, sugar, oil, salt, baking soda and baking powder. Use a rubber spatula to scrape down sides of blender. Lightly grease preheated griddle. Pour batter 1/2 cup or 1/4 cup at a time onto griddle. Bake pancakes only until dry 1/2 inch to 1 inch around edge. Turn with a pancake turner. Makes twelve 7-inch pancakes or twenty-four 3-inch pancakes.

Variations

Buttermilk Pancakes: Substitute 1 cup buttermilk for the milk.

Rolled Whole-Wheat Pancakes: Substitute 2 cups rolled whole-wheat for the whole-wheat kernels.

Rolled Oats Pancakes: Substitute 2-1/3 cups rolled oats for the whole-wheat kernels.

Cornmeal Pancakes: Substitute 1/2 cup cornmeal and 3/4 cup all-purpose flour for the whole-wheat kernels.

Beef-Flavored Gluten

A tasty and nourishing substitute for meat.

**7 cups whole-wheat flour from
  hard Winter wheat**

**3 cups cold water
Flavoring Broth, see below**

Flavoring Broth:
**2 cups hot water
1/2 cup chopped fresh onion
2 tablespoons beef-flavored
  bouillon granules**

**1 tablespoon soy sauce
1 teaspoon Worcestershire sauce
4 teaspoons seasoned salt**

In a large bowl, combine flour and 3 cups cold water, mixing with a spoon, then knead with your hands. Turn out on a floured surface. Pound ball of dough 10 minutes with a firm, flat object or knead and pound with your hands. Place pounded ball of dough in bowl. Cover with cold water and let stand 1 hour. Discard water or save to use in cooking. Cover dough with hot tap water. Gently press with your hands to wash starch and bran out of dough. Reserve water from this washing and the next to use in making soups, sauces or pancakes. Wash as many times as necessary until water remains clear. Cut resulting gluten ball into steaks, patties, balls, cubes or strips. Prepare Flavoring Broth. Add cut gluten pieces to broth. Simmer 30 minutes or until flavor has been absorbed. Drain. Makes 1-1/2 to 2 cups beef-flavored gluten.

Flavoring Broth:
In a large skillet, combine hot water, onion, bouillon granules, soy sauce, Worcestershire sauce and seasoned salt. Bring to a simmer.

Variations
Chicken-Flavored Gluten: Substitute chicken-flavored bouillon granules for beef-flavored bouillon granules.
Italian-Flavored Gluten: Add 1 teaspoon Italian seasoning to Flavoring Broth.

Peruvian Whole-Wheat Soup

Create a tasty wholesome soup with a few basic foods and flavorings.

**3/4 cup whole-wheat flour
4-1/2 cups canned or homemade beef broth
1-1/4 teaspoons salt**

**2 tablespoons dried chopped onion
1/2 teaspoon dried minced garlic
1/4 teaspoon dried leaf oregano, crushed**

In a 2-quart saucepan, brown flour about 10 minutes over medium heat, stirring constantly with a wooden spoon. Set aside to cool about 5 minutes. Gradually stir broth into browned flour. Stir in salt, onion and garlic. Cook and stir over low heat about 15 minutes until mixture thickens slightly. Soup should not be thick. Stir in oregano. Serve hot. Makes about 4 servings.

Variation
Before serving, stir in 1/2 cup shredded sharp Cheddar cheese.

Whole-Grain Patties

Add any leftover vegetables.

2 to 3 cups Slow-Cooked Wheat, page 96,
  or Thermos Wheat, page 96
1 medium potato, unpeeled, quartered
2 medium carrots, unpeeled, cut in pieces
1 onion, quartered
1/2 cup canned whole-kernel corn, drained
4 radishes
Radish leaves, if desired
2 tablespoons canned chopped green
  chilies, if desired

1 teaspoon salt
1/4 teaspoon seasoned salt
Pinch of garlic powder
1 teaspoon Worcestershire sauce
About 1/3 cup oil or bacon drippings
1 cup shredded Cheddar cheese (4 oz.)
Carroll's Salsa, page 68, or
  other salsa
2 tablespoons canned chopped green
  chilies, if desired

Prepare cooked wheat. Place a baking dish under food grinder. If using a hand grinder, place a medium bowl under handle to catch drippings. Grind together cooked wheat, potato, carrots, onion, corn, radishes and radish leaves, if desired. Grind chilies, if desired. Spoon ground mixture into a large bowl as baking dish fills. Stir in salt, seasoned salt, garlic powder, Worcestershire sauce and 2 tablespoons oil or bacon drippings. Lightly grease a griddle or skillet with oil or bacon drippings and place over medium heat. When hot, spoon 1/4 cup wheat mixture onto griddle. Flatten with a spatula to make patties. If patties stick, add 1 to 2 tablespoons oil or bacon drippings. Cook until lightly browned, then turn and brown other side. Place a little shredded cheese on each patty. Cook until cheese is melted. Repeat with remaining wheat mixture. Serve with Carroll's Salsa or other salsa. Makes 12 to 15 patties or 6 to 8 servings.

Wheat & Sausage Deep-Dish

This makes an excellent base for rice and beans. See the variation below.

2-1/2 cups Slow-Cooked Wheat, page 96,
  or Thermos Wheat, page 96
1/2 lb. pork sausage or Breakfast
  Sausage, page 26
1 medium onion, chopped
1/2 cup water
1/4 cup mixed dried chopped peppers

1/2 teaspoon seasoned salt
1/4 teaspoon black pepper
1/4 teaspoon garlic salt
1/4 teaspoon Italian seasoning
1 (16-oz.) can stewed tomatoes
1 cup tomato juice
1/4 cup shredded Longhorn cheese (1 oz.)

Prepare cooked wheat; set aside. Prepare Breakfast Sausage, if using. Brown sausage in a large skillet. Add onion. Cook over medium-low heat until tender. Stir in 1/2 cup water and peppers. Simmer 3 to 5 minutes until peppers have absorbed most of water. Stir in seasoned salt, black pepper, garlic salt, Italian seasoning, tomatoes and tomato juice. Stir in cooked wheat. Cover and simmer 10 to 15 minutes until wheat is hot. Turn into a large serving bowl. Sprinkle with cheese. Makes about 6 servings.

Variation

Stir 1 to 2 cups cooked rice into sausage mixture when cooked wheat is added.

How to Make Whole-Grain Patties

1/Grind together vegetables and cooked wheat.

2/Place shredded cheese on cooked side of each patty. Cook until cheese is melted.

Turkey Pilaf

A wonderful meal to make with leftover Roast Turkey, page 134.

2 cups Slow-Cooked Wheat, page 96, or
   Thermos Wheat, page 96
1/4 cup butter or margarine
1/2 cup chopped fresh onion
2 cups chopped cooked turkey
1/2 teaspoon celery seeds
1/2 teaspoon ground thyme

2 teaspoons dried leaf parsley
1/2 cup hot water
2 chicken bouillon cubes
1 (16-oz.) can tomatoes, drained, chopped
1/3 cup raisins or chopped,
   mixed dried fruit
1/4 cup chopped walnuts, if desired

Prepare cooked wheat; set aside. In a large skillet or saucepan, melt butter or margarine. Stir in onion. Sauté 2 minutes. Stir in turkey, celery seeds, thyme and parsley. Cook and stir about 5 minutes until turkey is lightly browned. In a small bowl, pour hot water over bouillon cubes. Stir to dissolve. Stir bouillon mixture, wheat, tomatoes and raisins or mixed fruit into turkey mixture. Add walnuts, if desired. Cover and bring to a boil. Simmer over medium-low heat 15 minutes. Do not stir. Serve immediately. Makes about 6 servings.

Polka-Dot Bread

Photo also on on page 52.

Whole kernels of cooked wheat give this wholesome bread a nutty flavor.

1 cup Slow-Cooked Wheat, page 96, or
   Thermos Wheat, page 96,
   drained well
2 cups warm water
1/4 cup honey
1 envelope active dry yeast
   (1 tablespoon)

2 teaspoons salt
1/3 cup instant or non-instant
   milk powder
1/4 cup vegetable shortening, melted
4-1/2 to 5-1/2 cups whole-wheat flour

Prepare cooked wheat; set aside. Pour water into a medium bowl. Stir in honey. Sprinkle yeast over surface. Let stand 5 to 10 minutes until foamy. Add salt, milk powder, melted shortening and 3 cups flour. Stir to combine, then beat until smooth. Stir in cooked wheat and enough remaining flour to make a stiff dough. Turn out onto a lightly floured surface. Cover and let rest 3 to 5 minutes. Clean and grease bowl. Knead dough 8 to 10 minutes, adding flour to surface as needed. Place kneaded dough in greased bowl, turning to grease all sides. Cover and let rise in a warm place until doubled in bulk. Grease two 9" x 5" loaf pans. Punch down dough. Divide dough in half. On lightly floured surface, press each half with your hands or roll with a rolling pin to a 14" x 7" rectangle. Beginning at 1 short end, roll tightly jelly-roll-fashion. Pinch edge and ends to seal. Place rolled dough seam-side up in prepared pans to grease top of rolls. Turn dough, placing seam-side down. Cover and let rise in a warm place until dough rises above top of pan. Preheat oven to 375F (190C). Bake loaves about 25 minutes until browned and loaves sound hollow when the bottoms are tapped with your fingers. Turn out of pans. Cool on a rack. Makes 2 loaves.

Diana's Peruvian Surprise Pudding

Everyone applauds the person who gets the remaining clove.

2-1/2 cups water
1/2 cup unsulfured molasses
1/4 cup packed dark brown sugar
4 whole cloves
1 cinnamon stick

1/2 cup whole-wheat flour
1/4 teaspoon ground cloves
1 teaspoon ground cinnamon
1-1/2 cups evaporated milk
1/3 cup raisins

In a large saucepan, combine water, molasses, brown sugar, whole cloves and cinnamon stick. Bring to a boil over medium heat. Boil gently 10 minutes to blend flavors and dissolve sugar. While syrup cooks, pour flour into a small bowl. Stir in ground cloves and ground cinnamon. Gradually stir in milk. Beat until smooth. Remove and discard 3 cloves and cinnamon stick from cooked syrup. Slowly stir flour mixture into cooked syrup. Cook and stir over low heat about 3 minutes until slightly thickened. Stir in raisins. Simmer 5 minutes over low heat, stirring occasionally. Spoon into 4 to 6 dessert dishes. Makes about 4 cups.

Polka-Dot Bread; Freezer Red Raspberry Jam, page 25; and English Lemon Curd, page 25

Next time you want to make a special dessert, reach into your cupboard, refrigerator or freezer for all the scrumptious ingredients. This is not luxury; it's the result of sound planning and wise purchases. For example, you might have saved several dollars by buying a quantity of sugar, nuts and canned fruit on sale 6 months ago. If you're in the mood for making a glorious dessert today, it makes no difference that you're short of time and money. You've already bought and stored everything you need! This is also the time to take advantage of dried milk and dried eggs or eggs stored in water glass.

Desserts

If it seems difficult to put by enough canned or frozen milk and you don't know how to store eggs in quantity, don't despair. Powdered nonfat milk is available in every major supermarket as well as in local grocery stores. It can be stored for 1 to 2 years. Dried eggs are available. You may have to buy them by the case from a dried-foods distributor. Fresh eggs will keep in water glass for several months. For information on water glassing eggs, see page 13.

Most recipes in this section have a little less sugar than you might expect. For both health and economy, we have attempted to reduce the sugar content of foods made with our recipes. In general, we have found the amount of sugar called for in most recipes outside this cookbook can be reduced by a fourth to a half without being noticed. In some recipes the texture may be affected slightly. If you wish to reduce sugar in a recipe, start by reducing it a few tablespoons at a time. Make a note on the recipe indicating the amount of sugar used. If you like the results, reduce the sugar by a few more tablespoons next time.

Sugar can be stored for years but it will absorb moisture and harden if it is not stored carefully. All varieties of sugar must be stored in airtight containers in a cool, dry place.

As you stock up for desserts, consider adding a few new and different spices. Replenish your spices before you run out. After 12 months, most spices begin to lose their flavor. Make a chart of all the spices in your cupboard and those in our list, page 156, that you plan to purchase. Begin a rotation system, replacing your spices within 12 to 18 months.

Extracts such as vanilla and almond lose their potency when exposed to air, so uncap them immediately before using and replace the caps as soon as you've measured what you need.

Do you have a whisk? It's a simple tool for mixing and blending. You'll find it indispensable once you've tried one. It works miracles smoothing a lumpy sauce or topping.

Wonderful dessert recipes are also in other recipe sections of this book. Look in Holidays, page 130, for holiday pies and other special desserts. Cookies & Candies start on page 146. For something different, try Diana's Peruvian Surprise Pudding in the Wheat section.

Family Celebration

Mandarin Soup, page 48
Corn & Asparagus Scallop, page 50
Mushroom Ramekins, page 50
Boiled Potatoes
Savory Pot Roast, page 82
Sunday-Best Chocolate Cake, page 116

Baked Fruit Whip

Try Stewed Fruit as a topping for breakfast cereal.

English Lemon Curd, page 25
Stewed Fruit, see below
1/3 cup sugar

1/3 cup chopped walnuts, if desired
4 egg whites or equivalent
3 tablespoons sugar

Stewed Fruit:
1 cup dried apricots or dried prunes
1 cup water

1 teaspoon grated lemon peel
3 tablespoons sugar

Prepare English Lemon Curd. Prepare Stewed Fruit. Preheat oven to 325F (165C). Lightly butter a 2-quart baking pan. Chop enough fruit to make 1-1/2 cups. Turn chopped fruit into a large bowl. Stir in 1/3 cup sugar. Add chopped walnuts, if desired. In a medium bowl, beat egg whites until stiff but not dry. Gradually beat in 3 tablespoons sugar. Fold beaten egg white mixture into fruit mixture. Spoon lightly into prepared baking pan. Bake 30 minutes. Remove fruit whip from oven. Cool on a rack 15 minutes. Spoon into 6 sherbet glasses or small dessert bowls. Serve hot or cold with lemon curd. Makes 6 servings.

Stewed Fruit:
In a medium bowl, soak apricots or prunes in water 4 hours or overnight. Pour fruit and water into a medium saucepan. Stir in lemon peel. Bring to a boil over medium-high heat. Simmer 15 minutes. Stir in 3 tablespoons sugar. Cook and stir 1 minute longer. Remove from heat. Cool on a rack. Remove pits from fruit. Store fruit in a glass jar with a tight-fitting lid until ready to use.

Spiced Flans

Rich Mexican custards with caramel topping are so good and so easy!

1/2 cup sugar
1 (14-oz.) can sweetened condensed milk
1 cup whole milk

4 eggs, beaten, or equivalent
1/4 teaspoon ground cinnamon

Heat sugar in a small heavy skillet over medium-high heat. When sugar begins to melt and brown, reduce heat to medium and begin stirring immediately. Continue stirring sugar frequently until it is melted and browned, or *caramelized*. Remove from heat and immediately spoon 1-1/2 tablespoons melted sugar into each of 6 custard cups. Set aside to cool. Preheat oven to 325F (165C). Combine condensed milk, whole milk, eggs and cinnamon in a blender. Process until thoroughly mixed. Pour equally into custard cups with caramel. Place in an 8-inch square baking pan. Pour hot water into pan halfway up sides of custard cups. Bake about 45 minutes until a knife inserted in center of a custard comes out clean. Remove custard cups from hot water. Set aside to cool. Refrigerate cool custards at least 1-1/2 hours. To serve, run a knife around custard in each cup. Invert onto a dessert plate and remove custard cup. Spoon any remaining caramel in cup onto top of custard. Makes 6 servings.

Melba Cobbler

Melba describes a dish where peaches and raspberries are used together.

1 (8-3/4-oz.) can sliced peaches,
  undrained
1 (10-oz.) pkg. frozen raspberries,
  thawed
1/3 cup packed brown sugar
3 tablespoons vegetable oil
1 cup all-purpose flour

1/2 teaspoon baking powder
1/2 teaspoon baking soda
2 tablespoons butter or margarine,
  cut in small pieces
1/2 cup walnut or pecan halves
Whipped Topping, page 118

Butter an 11'' x 7'' baking pan. Spread peaches and raspberries in bottom of prepared baking pan. Preheat oven to 350F (175C). Combine brown sugar and oil in a medium bowl; mix well. Sift together flour, baking powder and baking soda into brown sugar mixture. Cut in with a pastry blender to mix well. Spoon mixture evenly over fruit. Dot with butter or margarine pieces. Arrange walnut or pecan halves on batter. Bake 40 minutes. Cool slightly before serving. Prepare Whipped Topping just before serving. Serve cobbler with Whipped Topping. Makes 6 servings.

Ginger Peach-Berry Pie

The hint of ginger gives a special flavor to this fruit pie.

1 (29-oz.) can peach halves
1 tablespoon cornstarch
1/4 cup granulated brown sugar
Flaky Pie Pastry or Rich Pie Pastry for
  double-crust pie, page 113
1 tablespoon all-purpose flour

1 tablespoon dry tapioca
1 cup frozen blueberries,
  partially thawed
1/4 teaspoon ground ginger
1 tablespoon lemon juice or lime juice
About 1 teaspoon milk

Drain peach halves, reserving 1/3 cup syrup. Combine reserved syrup and cornstarch in a small saucepan; mix well. Add brown sugar. Whisk over low heat until thickened. Remove from heat and let cool. Prepare pastry. Roll out dough and line a 9-inch pie pan following directions on page 113. Sprinkle flour and dry tapioca over bottom of pastry to prevent a soggy crust. Arrange peach halves rounded-ends down in pastry-lined pan. Sprinkle with blueberries. Add ginger and lemon or lime juice to cornstarch mixture. Stir to mix well. Pour over peaches and blueberries. Preheat oven to 425F (220C). Roll out dough for top crust. Cut into 10 to 14 strips about 3/4 inch wide. Place 5 to 7 of the strips in 1 direction across top of pie but fold back instead of placing on top of filling. Place one of the remaining strips horizontally on 1 end of pie. Weave across pie with folded back strips. Repeat with remaining strips to make a lattice. Flute edges. Brush edges and lattice with milk. Bake about 30 minutes or until golden. Serve warm. Makes 8 servings.

How to Make Melba Cobbler

1/Spread peaches and raspberries in a baking pan. Combine brown sugar and oil.

2/Arrange brown sugar mixture over fruit. Dot with butter or margarine pieces.

Caribbean Bread Pudding

Bread pudding at its best, serve plain or top with milk or ice cream.

**1 (16-oz.) can tropical fruit salad,
  undrained
3 eggs or equivalent
Water
2/3 cup instant milk powder
1/2 cup packed brown sugar**

**1/2 teaspoon vanilla extract
1/4 teaspoon ground cinnamon
3 to 5 slices bread, toasted, buttered,
  cubed (3 cups)
1/2 cup raisins
2/3 cup dry roasted unsalted peanuts**

Drain fruit salad, reserving juice. In a medium bowl, beat eggs. Measure reserved juice from fruit salad; add water to measure 2-1/2 cups. Add to beaten eggs. Stir in milk powder, brown sugar, vanilla and cinnamon. In a 13" x 9" baking pan, layer half the toast cubes, half the raisins, half the peanuts and half the fruit salad. Repeat layers. Pour egg mixture over layers. Let stand 30 minutes. Preheat oven to 350F (175C). Bake 1-1/2 hours. Let stand about 10 minutes before serving. Makes 8 to 10 servings.

Lemon Meringue Cups

A perfect summer dessert for a patio dinner party.

3 egg whites or equivalent	1/2 teaspoon vanilla extract
1 cup sugar	1/2 teaspoon white vinegar
Pinch of salt	Lemon Cloud, see below

Lemon Cloud:

3 eggs, beaten, or equivalent	1/4 cup lemon juice
2/3 cup sugar	1 tablespoon grated lemon peel
Pinch of salt	Whipped Topping, page 118

Preheat oven to 300F (150C). In a large bowl, beat egg whites until soft peaks form. Gradually beat in sugar and salt until stiff peaks form. Beat in vanilla and vinegar. Cover a large baking sheet with brown paper. Spoon or pipe egg white mixture onto brown paper in 6 to 8 mounds. Use the back of a metal spoon to flatten and shape mounds into 3-inch round cups, making outer edges slightly thicker than centers. Bake 1 hour. Turn off oven. Let meringues cool in closed oven about 1 hour. Prepare Lemon Cloud. Spoon evenly into cooled meringues. Place on a large baking sheet. Store in freezer at least 1 hour before serving. Makes 6 to 8 servings.

Lemon Cloud:
In the top of a double boiler, combine eggs, sugar, salt and lemon juice. Cook and stir over simmering water until thickened. Stir in lemon peel. Cool to room temperature. Prepare Whipped Topping. Fold into egg mixture.

Variation
Frosty Cherry Meringue Cups: Fill meringue cups with Cherry Ice Cream, page 117, and serve with Cherry Sauce, below.

Cherry Sauce

Add extra color and flavor to ice cream, pancakes or pudding.

1 (16-oz.) jar maraschino cherries	Pinch of salt
1 cup water	1/4 teaspoon cherry flavoring
2 to 3 tablespoons all-purpose flour	3 to 5 drops red food coloring

Drain cherries, reserving liquid in a small saucepan. Chop cherries and set aside. In a small bowl, stir 2 to 4 tablespoons water into flour and salt, making a thin paste. Add remaining water to reserved liquid. Stir in flour-paste mixture. Stir over medium-high heat until mixture thickens slightly. Stir in cherry flavoring and red food coloring. Stir in about 1/4 cup cherries. Reserve remaining cherries for another use. Cook and stir 30 seconds longer. Makes about 1-1/2 cups.

Frosty Cherry Meringue Cups and Cherry Sauce

Apple Upside-Down Pie

This pie is best when made in a cast-iron skillet.

1 (20-oz.) can sliced apples
Flaky Pie Pastry or Rich Pie Pastry for
   single-crust pie, page 113
1/2 cup sugar

1/3 to 1/2 cup chopped walnuts
1/4 teaspoon ground cinnamon
1/4 teaspoon grated lemon peel

Drain apple slices, reserving juice. Prepare pastry dough using juice from apples in place of water. Roll out dough to a 9-1/2-inch circle. Trim to make edges neat. Preheat oven to 425F (220C). Heat sugar in a heavy 8-inch skillet with an ovenproof handle. When sugar begins to melt and brown, reduce heat to medium and stir immediately. Continue stirring frequently until sugar is melted and brown, or *caramelized*. Remove from heat. Immediately sprinkle chopped walnuts onto caramelized sugar. Arrange drained apple slices in skillet to make an even layer. Sprinkle with cinnamon and lemon peel. Roll pie dough over rolling pin to transfer to skillet and place over apples. Trim dough to fit skillet. Use a knife to cut three 1-inch slits in dough to let steam escape while cooking. Bake 30 to 35 minutes until crust is browned. Let pie cool 1 to 2 minutes. Place a round platter or large plate upside-down over skillet. Invert plate and skillet. Remove skillet, scraping out any nuts and apples that remain on the bottom. Cut into wedges and serve. Makes 4 to 6 servings.

Strawberry-Rhubarb Cream

Yogurt adds a luxurious creaminess with few calories.

1 cup frozen unsweetened cut rhubarb
1 cup water
1/4 cup sugar
1 (3-oz.) pkg. strawberry-flavored gelatin

1 cup boiling water
1 cup Homemade Yogurt, page 18, or
   plain yogurt

Combine rhubarb, 1 cup water and sugar in a small saucepan. Bring to a boil. Simmer uncovered over medium heat until rhubarb is very soft, 10 to 15 minutes. Set aside to cool. Dissolve gelatin in boiling water. Let cool to room temperature. Combine cooled rhubarb and juice, cooled gelatin mixture and yogurt in a blender or food processor. Process until smooth. Pour into dessert dishes. Refrigerate until set, 1 to 2 hours. Makes 4 to 6 servings.

How to Make Apple Upside-Down Pie

1/Stir sugar frequently until it is melted and browned.

2/Sprinkle walnuts over sugar and arrange apple slices on top.

3/Roll pie dough over rolling pin. Unroll dough over apples in skillet.

4/Invert skillet onto a plate, then remove skillet.

Almond Fruit Tartlets

Enjoy these delectable pastries year round.

English Lemon Curd, page 25
Apricot Filling, see below
Rich Pie Pastry for double-crust pie,
    page 113

6 to 12 almonds, finely chopped
Whipped Topping, page 118

Apricot Filling:
1 (6-oz.) pkg. dried apricots
1 cup water

1/2 cup sugar
1/2 teaspoon almond extract

Prepare English Lemon Curd, Apricot Filling and Rich Pie Pastry. Roll out pastry. Place 2-inch tartlet pans upside down on dough. With a knife, cut around each pan. Press dough cutout into each pan with your fingers, trimming edges if necessary. Prick bottom of each shell 3 times with a fork. Preheat oven to 450F (230C). Place pans with shells on baking sheets. Bake 8 to 10 minutes or until golden. Remove from oven. Let cool slightly. Remove shells from pans and place on a plate. Fill half the shells with lemon curd. Fill remaining shells with Apricot Filling. Sprinkle chopped almonds over fillings. Prepare Whipped Topping just before serving. Top each tartlet with Whipped Topping. Makes about 32 tartlets.

Apricot Filling:
Place apricots, water and sugar in a medium saucepan. Bring to a boil; reduce heat. Cover and simmer 15 minutes. Remove from heat. Mash apricots. Mixture should be lumpy. Let cool about 5 minutes. Stir in almond extract.

Rich Milk

Use this mixture in any recipe calling for sweetened condensed milk.

1-1/2 cups fine-grain instant milk powder
1/2 cup water
3/4 cup sugar

1 tablespoon butter-flavor granules,
    if desired

Combine milk powder and water in a medium saucepan. Let stand 15 minutes, beating occasionally until smooth. Stir in sugar and butter-flavor granules, if desired. Stir mixture over medium heat until bubbling, about 4 minutes. Reduce heat and stir over low heat about 5 minutes or until mixture is smooth. Makes 1 to 1-1/2 cups.

Flaky Pie Pastry

A fool-proof recipe for superb pastry.

2 cups all-purpose flour
1/2 teaspoon salt

10 tablespoons shortening
7 to 8 tablespoons water

Combine flour and salt in a medium bowl. Cut in shortening with a pastry blender or 2 knives until mixture resembles small peas. Sprinkle with 7 tablespoons water. Stir until mixture forms a ball and leaves side of bowl. Add more water if needed. Turn out dough onto a lightly floured surface. Knead 10 to 15 times. Divide dough into 2 equal portions. Roll out 1 portion to a 12-inch circle. Fold in half, then in half again. Place in a 9-inch pie pan with folded corner in middle of pan. Unfold dough. Gently ease into pan; trim edge 1/2 inch larger than pan. Fill with prepared pie filling. Roll out and fold remaining dough as directed above. Cut small slashes about 1-1/2 inches from point. Place folded dough over filling with folded corner at center. Gently unfold dough. Trim edge 1 inch larger than pan. Fold upper crust under lower crust. Flute edge. Makes pastry for one 9-inch double-crust pie.

Rich Pie Pastry

Wonderful pastry for either sweet or savory dishes!

2 cups all-purpose flour
1 teaspoon sugar
1/4 teaspoon salt
1/2 cup vegetable shortening

1/3 cup butter or margarine
1 teaspoon white vinegar
1 egg, beaten, or equivalent
3 tablespoons water

Combine flour, sugar and salt in a large bowl. Cut in shortening and butter or margarine with a pastry blender or 2 knives until mixture resembles small peas. Combine vinegar, egg and water in a small bowl; stir with a fork. Add to flour mixture and mix well with fork to make a smooth dough. Shape into a ball. Follow instructions for Flaky Pie Pastry, above, to roll out dough. Makes enough pastry for one 9-inch double-crust pie.

Both these pie-crust recipes are for double-crust pies. Halve the recipes to make single-crust pies. If you're making a single-crust Rich Pie Pastry, use 1-1/2 to 2 tablespoons beaten egg or the equivalent for half a beaten egg.

Pastry freezes well. After you have shaped the dough into a ball, wrap tightly in plastic wrap. Then place it in a freezer bag and secure it with a twist tie or wrap it again in freezer wrap. Be sure to label it. Pastry can be kept frozen 5 to 6 months. To thaw, let the dough stand in the refrigerator overnight or at room temperature for several hours.

Chocolate Fondue

Apple wedges and banana slices make good dippers also.

All-Occasion White Cake, below, or
    graham crackers
2/3 cup unsweetened cocoa powder
2/3 cup sugar
Pinch of salt

1/2 cup water
1/4 teaspoon vanilla extract
Marshmallows
Maraschino cherries
Pineapple chunks

Prepare All-Occasion White Cake, if using. Cut into bite-size pieces. Arrange on a platter or serving dish. Combine cocoa powder, sugar and salt in a fondue pot, chafing dish or double boiler. Stir in water gradually. Use a whisk if necessary to break up lumps. Bring to a boil over medium-low heat, stirring frequently. Reduce heat to low. Simmer 2 minutes, stirring frequently. Stir in vanilla. With a fondue fork, dip fruit, cake or marshmallows into chocolate mixture. Crackers may be broken in small squares and dipped by hand. Leftover fondue can be refrigerated for several days or served as a dessert sauce. Makes 6 to 8 servings.

All-Occasion White Cake

Wonderful for dipping into Chocolate Fondue.

1 cup milk
1 teaspoon vanilla extract
1/4 cup butter or margarine,
    room temperature

1-1/4 cups sugar
3 eggs, beaten, or equivalent
3 cups Basic Baking Mix, page 121

Butter a 15-1/2" x 10-1/2" jelly-roll pan. Preheat oven to 350F (175C). In a 1-cup measure, combine milk and vanilla; set aside. In a large bowl, beat butter or margarine until smooth. Gradually beat in sugar. Add one-third of the beaten eggs at a time, beating well after each addition. Stir in 2 cups Basic Baking Mix. Stir in 1/2 cup milk mixture. Beat with electric mixer 2 minutes until smooth and thick. Beat in remaining Basic Baking Mix and remaining milk mixture. Beat 1 minute. Pour into prepared pan. Bake 22 to 25 minutes or until a wooden pick inserted in center comes out clean. Makes 1 sheet cake.

Variations

All-Occasion Layer Cake: Bake batter in two 8-inch, round cake pans. Fill with English Lemon Curd, page 25, or Freezer Raspberry Jam, page 25. Frost with Sunday-Best Chocolate Frosting, page 116, or Whipped Topping, page 118.

All-Occasion Chocolate Cake: Melt 2 (1-ounce) squares unsweetened chocolate. Beat into batter with eggs.

Sunday-Best Chocolate Cake

For a children's party or picnic, make the cupcake variation below.

1/2 cup butter or margarine,
   room temperature
1-1/2 cups sugar
2 eggs or equivalent
1-1/2 cups water
1 teaspoon vanilla extract

2-1/4 cups all-purpose flour
6 tablespoons unsweetened cocoa powder
1/2 teaspoon salt
1 teaspoon baking soda
6 tablespoons buttermilk powder
Sunday-Best Chocolate Frosting, below

Butter and flour 2 round, 8-inch cake pans. Preheat oven to 350F (175C). Cream together butter or margarine and sugar in a large bowl. Beat in eggs. Combine water and vanilla in a 2-cup measure. Combine flour, cocoa powder, salt, baking soda and buttermilk powder. Sift onto a 12-inch square of waxed paper or into a medium bowl. Beat about one-third of the sifted flour mixture into egg mixture. Beat in half the water mixture. Beat in another one-third of the flour mixture and remaining water mixture. Stir in remaining flour mixture. Combine thoroughly. Divide batter between prepared cake pans. Bake 25 minutes or until a wooden pick inserted in centers of cakes comes out clean. Turn out of cake pans onto racks to cool. Prepare Sunday-Best Chocolate Frosting. Fill and frost cooled cake. Makes 8 to 10 servings.

Variation

Sunday-Best Chocolate Cupcakes: Bake batter in lined muffin cups 20 minutes. Makes 24 to 30 cupcakes.

Sunday-Best Chocolate Frosting

Smooth and velvety, this frosting is spreadable on any cake or cookie.

3 cups powdered sugar
3 tablespoons unsweetened cocoa powder
Pinch of salt
1/4 cup butter or margarine,
   room temperature

1 egg, beaten, or equivalent
2 to 4 tablespoons half and half or
   evaporated milk
1 teaspoon vanilla extract

Sift together powdered sugar, cocoa and salt into a large bowl. Add remaining ingredients, increasing half and half or evaporated milk as needed. Beat until smooth. Use to frost cakes or cookies. Makes about 1-1/2 cups.

Grandma's Secret Ice Cream

For best results, use real vanilla extract and real lemon extract.

2 cups sugar	1 (13-oz.) can evaporated milk
3/4 teaspoon salt	2 tablespoons vanilla extract
1/4 cup all-purpose flour	2 teaspoons lemon extract
1-1/2 cups instant milk powder	About 4-1/2 cups whole milk
4 cups water	Rock salt
4 eggs, beaten, or equivalent	Crushed ice

In a large saucepan, combine sugar, salt, flour and milk powder. Gradually stir in water. Stir in eggs until mixture is blended. Cook, stirring constantly over low heat until mixture thickens enough to coat a metal spoon, 15 to 20 minutes. Pour into a large bowl. Refrigerate 1 hour or until chilled. Stir in evaporated milk, vanilla and lemon extract. Pour into ice cream canister. Stir in enough whole milk to raise mixture to fill line. Freeze in ice cream maker according to manufacturer's instructions using 1 cup of rock salt to about 8 cups crushed ice. Makes 1 gallon.

Variations

Cherry Ice Cream: *Photo on page 109.*
When ice cream is partially frozen, remove lid and add 1 to 1-1/2 cups chopped maraschino cherries. Continue freezing. Serve with Cherry Sauce, page 108.

Strawberry Ice Cream: Puree 2 cups strawberries. Stir into chilled egg mixture before freezing in ice cream maker. Reduce vanilla extract to 1 tablespoon.

Chocolate Swirl Ice Cream: When ice cream is frozen, remove lid and dasher. Insert a long wooden spoon. Pour cooled Choc-P-Nutty Sauce, below, into ice cream next to spoon. Draw spoon back and forth through ice cream several times to distribute sauce. If sauce is too thick to swirl, stir in 2 to 3 tablespoons evaporated milk before adding to ice cream.

Choc-P-Nutty Sauce

Delicious served over ice cream or cake.

1 cup sugar	1/4 cup butter or margarine
1 tablespoon all-purpose flour	2 rounded tablespoons chunky
Pinch of salt	peanut butter
2 tablespoons unsweetened cocoa powder	1/4 teaspoon vanilla extract
3/4 cup evaporated milk	

In a small saucepan, combine sugar, flour, salt and cocoa powder. Blend mixture thoroughly. Stir in evaporated milk. Add butter or margarine. Stir over medium-high heat until mixture comes to a boil. Reduce heat to medium. Continue to stir and cook until mixture is slightly thickened, about 3 minutes. Remove from heat. Stir in peanut butter and vanilla. Serve hot or cold. Makes about 1-1/2 cups.

Gingerbread

Flavor and texture of Gingerbread improves if it is kept tightly wrapped for a few days.

1/3 cup butter or margarine,
   room temperature
1/2 cup sugar
2/3 cup unsulfured molasses
2 cups all-purpose flour
1 tablespoon baking powder

1/2 teaspoon baking soda
1/2 teaspoon salt
2 teaspoons ground ginger
1 teaspoon ground cinnamon
1/4 teaspoon ground cloves
1 cup sour milk or buttermilk

Preheat oven to 350F (175C). Lightly butter a 13" x 9" baking pan. Line bottom of pan with waxed paper; butter paper. In a medium bowl, cream together butter or margarine and sugar. Stir in molasses. Sift together flour, baking powder, baking soda, salt, ginger, cinnamon and cloves into a medium bowl. Stir sifted flour mixture into creamed mixture alternately with sour milk or buttermilk. Turn into prepared baking pan. Bake 30 to 35 minutes or until a wooden pick inserted in center comes out clean. Cool in pan on a rack, then place rack over pan. Invert cake onto rack; peel off waxed paper immediately. Makes 12 to 15 servings.

Whipped Topping

At last, a dessert topping that's economical, easy and low-calorie!

1/2 cup ice-cold water
1/2 cup instant milk powder

2 tablespoons lemon juice
1/3 cup sugar

Place a medium bowl and beaters in the freezer 15 minutes. In the cold bowl, combine water and milk powder. Beat with cold beaters until stiff peaks form. Gradually add lemon juice. Fold in sugar. Use immediately. Makes about 1-1/2 cups.

When you buy molasses for storage, choose the unsulfured variety. The taste of sulfur intensifies with long-term storage.

Flour, yeast, shortening or vegetable oil, sugar and dry milk are all you need to store to make basic breads. With baking powder, baking soda, molasses, honey and dried eggs or water-glass eggs, page 13, you can expand your bread repertoire to include a variety of quick breads. Add other ingredients such as fruit, vegetables, cornmeal and rolled oats for a different loaf every day of the month!

A loaf of homebaked bread is inexpensive and is delicious served with soup, pages 39 to 48, or salad, pages 53 to 56. Add protein to bread with peanut butter or a cheese spread. Both are easy to store at room temperature.

Whole-wheat flour and other whole-grain flours that still contain the germ and oil may become rancid if not stored in a cool, dry place. These flours should be used within 6 months.

When the germ and oil are removed, flour can be stored for a longer period. All-purpose flour does not contain the germ and oil. It should be kept in a cool, dry place and can be stored for as long as 2 years.

If you rarely use flour but like to keep it on hand for occasional breads and cakes, store the opened package in an airtight canister in your freezer. Several hours before baking, measure the amount of flour you need. Cover the flour and let it come to room temperature before using.

Active dry yeast is better suited to long storage than compressed cake yeast. Dry yeast has a lower moisture content and is less likely to dry out in storage. You can buy packages containing 1 tablespoon of dry yeast or larger quantities of dry yeast in jars or cans. It will keep unopened as long as 1 year in a cool place. It can be stored tightly covered or unopened in the freezer 2 years.

If you add dry yeast to liquid as directed by the recipe and the mixture does not foam within a few minutes, stir in 1 teaspoon of sugar. Wait 3 to 5 minutes longer. If the mixture does not foam, the yeast is no longer active. Discard the mixture and use another package of yeast or yeast from a different container.

If you bake bread and freeze it, remember bread doesn't keep its quality forever. Frozen yeast breads should be used within 4 to 6 months. Use frozen quick breads within 2 to 3 months.

One of the most important recipes in this book from a storage standpoint is Basic Baking Mix. It's used to make muffins, biscuits, breads, cakes, pancakes and pizza.

Basic Baking Mix is made with all-purpose flour. If you want to raise the nutritional content of baked goods, stir a spoonful or two of wheat germ into the Mix as you use it in recipes.

Breads

A loaf of white bread made with all-purpose enriched flour is nutritious. But you can boost the nutritional quality still more by substituting a few spoonfuls of whole-wheat flour for an equal amount of the all-purpose flour.

Delicious breads can be made from whole-wheat kernels. Cooked whole-wheat kernels can be kneaded into white bread dough to make Polka Dot Bread. See page 96 for methods of cooking whole-wheat kernels.

Sunday Morning Open House

Orange Fruit Molds, page 56
Raisin Bread Special, page 120
Refrigerated Rolls, page 123
Cinnamon Coffeecake, page 122
Honey Butter, page 25
Freezer Red Raspberry Jam, page 25
Dutch Honey, page 27
English Lemon Curd, page 25
Coffee and Herb Tea

Raisin Bread Special

Small round loaves add eye appeal to a tray of snacks.

2 cups boiling water
1 lb. seedless raisins
1/2 cup butter or margarine,
  room temperature
1-1/2 cups sugar
2 eggs, beaten, or equivalent

1 teaspoon vanilla extract
4 cups all-purpose flour
1 teaspoon salt
2 teaspoons baking soda
1/2 cup chopped walnuts, if desired

Collect 5 empty cans similar to 16-ounce vegetable cans; set aside. In a medium bowl, pour boiling water over raisins. Let stand overnight. Grease insides of 5 cans. Cut five 7'' x 6'' pieces of waxed paper. Grease 1 side of each paper. Make a tube of each greased waxed paper, rolling greased side in. Carefully insert into can, spreading tube to fit against sides. Repeat with remaining waxed paper and cans. Preheat oven to 350F (175C). In a large bowl, beat butter or margarine and sugar until creamy. Beat in eggs and vanilla. Stir in raisins with water. Sift together flour, salt and baking soda into raisin mixture. Add walnuts, if desired. Stir until mixed well. Spoon evenly into prepared cans, filling each can at least two-thirds full. Bake 1 hour. Remove from oven. Let cool 10 minutes on a rack. Remove bread and waxed paper from cans. Remove waxed paper from bread. Serve warm or cold. Makes 5 small loaves.

Winter-Squash Bread

For another delicious bread, substitute canned pumpkin or yams.

2/3 cup vegetable shortening
1-1/2 cups sugar
2 eggs, beaten, or equivalent
1-3/4 cups cooked, mashed winter squash
1/3 cup unsulfured molasses
4 cups all-purpose flour
1 teaspoon baking powder
1/2 teaspoon baking soda

1/2 teaspoon salt
1 tablespoon ground cinnamon
1/4 teaspoon ground ginger
1/2 teaspoon ground cloves
1/2 teaspoon grated lemon peel
2/3 cup milk
1 cup chopped walnuts or pecans,
  if desired

Grease two 9'' x 5'' loaf pans. Line each greased pan with waxed paper, letting paper extend 2 to 3 inches above long sides of pans. Preheat oven to 350F (175C). In a large bowl, cream together shortening and sugar. Beat in eggs, squash and molasses. In a medium bowl, combine flour, baking powder, baking soda, salt, cinnamon, ginger, cloves and lemon peel. Stir flour mixture and milk alternately into squash mixture, beginning and ending with flour mixture. Stir in walnuts or pecans, if desired. Pour into prepared loaf pans. Bake about 1 hour until golden brown. Turn out of pans; cool on a rack. Makes 2 loaves.

Basic Baking Mix

Use this handy mix for Busy Morning Pancakes & Waffles, page 31.

9 cups all-purpose flour
1/3 cup baking powder
1 cup plus 2 tablespoons instant or
  non-instant milk powder

4 teaspoons salt
1-3/4 cups vegetable shortening

In a large bowl, combine flour, baking powder, milk powder and salt, stirring to mix well. Cut in shortening with 2 knives or work in with your fingers until mixture resembles coarse crumbs. Store at room temperature in a tightly covered container for 4 to 6 months, or in the freezer up to 1 year. Stir lightly before measuring. Do not pack down in measuring cup. Level with a straight-edge spatula. Makes 13 cups.

Variations

Substitute 1-1/2 cups lard for 1-3/4 cups vegetable shortening. Store according to directions on lard wrapper.

Large-Quantity Basic Baking Mix: Use the amounts of ingredients as follows:

10 lbs. all-purpose flour
1-1/3 cups baking powder
4-1/2 cups instant or non-instant milk powder
5 tablespoons salt
1 (3-lb.) can vegetable shortening

Combine as directed above. Store in a large tightly covered container.

Country Biscuits

Vary your biscuits by adding nuts, raisins or other chopped fruit.

2 cups Basic Baking Mix, above
1/2 cup water or milk

Preheat oven to 425F (220C). Measure Basic Baking Mix into a medium bowl. Stir in water or milk until mixed well. Turn out on a lightly floured board. Knead about 15 times. Roll out 1/2 inch thick. Cut with a floured biscuit cutter or top of a 2-1/2-inch wide drinking glass. Arrange on an ungreased baking sheet. Bake 10 minutes. Makes about 12 biscuits.

Variations

Bacon Biscuits: Add 1/4 cup crumbled, crisp-cooked bacon to dry Mix.

Cheese Biscuits: Stir 1/3 cup shredded cheese or 1/2 cup Cheddar cheese powder into dry Mix.

Drop Biscuits: Increase liquid to 2/3 cup. Do not knead or roll dough. Drop by spoonfuls onto a greased baking sheet or into greased muffin cups. Also use as dumplings.

Cinnamon Coffeecake

There won't be any latecomers to the breakfast table when this is served!

Cinnamon-Sugar Topping, see below
2 cups Basic Baking Mix, page 121
1/3 cup sugar

1 egg, beaten, or equivalent
1 teaspoon vanilla extract
1/2 cup water or milk

Cinnamon-Sugar Topping:
1/4 cup granulated sugar
1/4 cup packed brown sugar
2 tablespoons Basic Baking Mix, page 121

1 teaspoon ground cinnamon
3 tablespoons butter or margarine

Prepare Cinnamon-Sugar Topping. Butter an 8- or 9-inch square baking pan. Preheat oven to 375F (190C). In a medium bowl, combine Basic Baking Mix and sugar. Stir egg and vanilla into water or milk. Stir egg mixture into dry ingredients until mixed well. Spread half the batter in bottom of prepared baking pan. Sprinkle evenly with half the topping. Spoon remaining batter evenly over topping. Sprinkle with remaining topping. Bake about 20 minutes. Makes 6 to 8 servings.

Cinnamon-Sugar Topping:
In a small bowl, combine sugars, Mix and cinnamon until blended. Cut in butter or margarine with 2 knives or press in with a fork.

How to Make Cinnamon Coffeecake

1/If using dried whole eggs, stir them into dry ingredients before adding liquid, page 14.

2/Spread half the batter in pan and sprinkle with half the topping. Cover with remaining batter and sprinkle with remaining topping.

Refrigerated Rolls   *Photo on cover and page 79.*

Delightfully light whether baked the same day or 5 days after you make the dough.

4-1/2 to 5 cups all-purpose flour
2 envelopes active dry yeast
   (2 tablespoons)
2 teaspoons salt
1/4 cup sugar

2/3 cup instant or non-instant
   milk powder
2 cups warm water
1/4 cup shortening, melted
2 eggs, beaten, or equivalent

In a large bowl, combine 2-1/2 cups flour, yeast, salt, sugar and powdered milk. Stir to mix well. Stir in warm water, shortening and eggs. Let stand 10 minutes. Beat 100 strokes by hand or about 2 minutes with an electric mixer. Stir in by hand, 1-1/2 cups flour. Stir in enough of remaining flour to make a medium-stiff dough. On a lightly floured board, knead 8 to 10 minutes until smooth with small bubbles under surface. Add more flour to board as needed. **To bake in 2 to 24 hours,** cover and let dough rest on board about 20 minutes. Grease 2 large baking sheets. Punch down dough. Shape into rolls according to variations below. Place 2 to 3 inches apart on prepared baking sheets. Cover rolls loosely with plastic wrap or foil. Refrigerate 2 to 24 hours. Carefully uncover rolls. Let stand at room temperature 10 minutes. Preheat oven to 375F (190C). Bake rolls 20 to 23 minutes until evenly browned. Remove from pans; cool on racks. **To bake in 2 to 5 days,** grease a 2-quart container with a tight-fitting lid. Place kneaded dough in container, turning to grease all sides. Refrigerate 2 to 5 days. When ready to use, turn dough out on a lightly floured board. Let rest 30 minutes. Shape into rolls according to variations below. Let rolls rise 30 minutes. Bake 23 to 25 minutes according to directions above. Makes about 48 rolls.

Variations

Pan Rolls: Pinch off pieces of dough about the size of medium eggs. Using your fingers, carefully tuck edges of dough to bottom of roll. Dip smooth top of roll in melted butter or margarine. Arrange rounded-side up in greased 9-inch round baking pans.

Rosettes: Roll out half the dough into a rectangle 1/4 inch thick. Cut rolled dough into 12" x 1" strips. Place 1 end of strip around your index finger. Holding other end of dough in your other hand, wind dough around your finger. Dough will twist. Pull your finger out of center. Tuck end of dough under roll. Arrange rolls tucked-end down in greased muffin cups.

Crescents: Roll out half the dough into a circle 1/4 inch thick. Cut dough into wedges, about 3 inches wide on outer edge. Roll each wedge jelly-roll-fashion from outer edge to point. Arrange on a greased baking sheet, with point under roll. Curve ends of roll to make crescents.

Pull Throughs: Roll out dough 1/4 inch thick. Cut in 3- to 4-inch circles. Make a 2-inch slash on 1 side of each dough circle following the curve of the circle. Use your fingers to pull the opposite side of the circle tightly through the slash. Arrange on a greased baking sheet.

Double Twists: Roll out half the dough to a 12" x 8" rectangle. Brush with melted butter or margarine. Fold in half lengthwise. Use a sharp knife or scissors to cut dough in 1/2- to 1-inch crosswise strips. From folded end, twist 2 sides of strip around each other. Pinch ends together. Arrange as sticks or in circles on a greased baking sheet.

Parker House Rolls: Roll out half the dough 1/4 inch thick. Cut into circles with a biscuit cutter or top of a small glass. Cut almost through centers of circles with blunt side of a knife. Brush top of each scored circle with melted butter or margarine. Fold circle in half with buttered surface inside. Arrange on a greased baking sheet.

Any of the rolls may be sprinkled with poppy seeds or sesame seeds after they are shaped.

If using dried eggs, stir them into flour mixture. Add water needed to rehydrate eggs to the 2 cups warm water and shortening. Continue as directed.

Breads

Dinner Casserole Loaf

Save time with a dough that has to rise only once.

3/4 cup warm water
1/2 teaspoon sugar
1 envelope active dry yeast
  (1 tablespoon)
1 cup ricotta cheese or cottage cheese
  (8 oz.)
1 egg, beaten, or equivalent
1 teaspoon salt
1/4 cup vegetable oil

1/2 teaspoon celery seeds
1/4 teaspoon celery salt
1 teaspoon dried leaf rosemary, crushed
3/4 teaspoon dried leaf basil, crushed
2 tablespoons dried minced onion,
  if desired
2-1/2 to 3 cups all-purpose flour
1/4 teaspoon celery seeds

Generously grease a deep, round 1-1/2-quart casserole with straight sides; set aside. In a large bowl, combine warm water and sugar. Sprinkle yeast over surface. Let stand 5 to 10 minutes until foamy. In a small saucepan, heat ricotta cheese or cottage cheese until warmed throughout. Stir until smooth. Set aside to cool slightly. Stir in egg, salt, oil, 1/2 teaspoon celery seeds, celery salt, rosemary and basil. Add onion, if desired. Stir cheese mixture into yeast mixture until blended. Stir in 2-1/2 cups flour until blended. Add more flour if needed to make a soft dough. Turn out onto a lightly floured surface. Knead gently about 5 minutes. Dough will be very soft, but not sticky. Place in prepared casserole, turning to grease all sides. Sprinkle with 1/4 teaspoon celery seeds. Cover and let rise in a warm place until doubled in bulk, about 45 minutes. Preheat oven to 425F (220C). Place raised dough in oven. Bake 10 minutes. Reduce heat to 350F (175C). Bake 15 to 20 minutes longer until loaf is golden brown and sounds hollow when the bottom is tapped with your fingers. Turn out of casserole onto a rack. Cool right-side-up 10 to 15 minutes before cutting with a serrated knife. Makes 1 large loaf.

Yorkshire Parkin

Popular in England for afternoon tea.

1-1/3 cups rolled oats
3/4 cup whole-wheat flour
1/2 teaspoon baking soda
1/2 teaspoon ground ginger
1/8 teaspoon ground allspice
1/2 cup raisins

1/3 cup packed brown sugar
1/2 cup unsulfured molasses
1/4 cup butter or margarine
1 egg, beaten, or equivalent
1 cup milk

Preheat oven to 350F (175C). Butter an 8-inch-square baking pan. In a large bowl, combine rolled oats, flour, baking soda, ginger, allspice and raisins. Mix well. In a small saucepan, heat brown sugar, molasses and butter or margarine over low heat until butter or margarine is melted. Beat egg and milk together in a small bowl. Add egg mixture to molasses mixture. Stir into flour mixture. Mix well. Turn batter into prepared pan. Bake 1 hour. Cool in pan on a rack 20 minutes. Cut into bars. Makes 10 to 16 bars.

Clockwise starting at the top, Yorkshire Parkin; Honey Butter, page 25; Spicy Beet Bread, page 128; and Dinner Casserole Loaf.

French Bread *Photo on page 45.*

After shaping, bake 1 loaf and freeze the other.

2 cups warm water
1/2 teaspoon sugar
1 envelope active dry yeast
 (1 tablespoon)

2 teaspoons salt
2 tablespoons vegetable oil
4 to 4-1/2 cups all-purpose flour
2 tablespoons cornmeal

In a large bowl, combine water and sugar. Sprinkle yeast over surface. Let stand 5 to 10 minutes until foamy. Stir in salt, oil and 2-1/2 cups flour. Beat 100 strokes by hand or 2 minutes with mixer. Stir in enough remaining flour to make a stiff sticky dough. Cover with a wet cloth and let rise in a warm place until doubled in bulk, about 1 hour. Grease a large baking sheet; sprinkle with cornmeal. Stir down dough. Turn out half the dough onto a floured board. Sprinkle dough with flour if needed. Roll out to a 12-inch square. Roll up from 1 side jelly-roll-fashion. Dampen edges with water if necessary to pinch and seal ends. Shape ends to make them narrow and rounded. Repeat with remaining dough. Place loaves side-by-side on prepared baking sheet. Use a sharp knife to cut 3 diagonal slashes across top of each loaf. Cover and let rise in a warm place until almost doubled in bulk. Preheat oven to 425F (220C). Use a pastry brush to brush water over tops and sides of loaves. Bake loaves 12 minutes. Reduce heat to 325F (165C). Again brush tops of loaves with water. Bake 35 minutes longer until browned and firm to the touch. Cool on a rack. **To freeze unbaked loaves:** shape loaves and arrange on baking sheet. Place uncovered loaves in freezer on baking sheet until firm, about 2 hours. Wrap each loaf in heavy foil or freezer wrap, making an airtight seal. Store in freezer; use within 2 months. **To bake frozen loaves:** Sprinkle cornmeal on a large baking sheet. Place frozen loaves on cornmeal. Cover with plastic wrap and let thaw, about 2 hours. Then let rise in a warm place until doubled in bulk. Bake as directed. Makes 2 loaves.

Vacuum-Packing Food for Storage

Food has been vacuum-packed by the food industry for many years. Recently, smaller machines suitable for vacuum-packing in the home have become available. There is a wide range in the price of the machines. They are available in several different designs. Investigate them all carefully to be sure the one you buy meets all your needs.

Easy Muffins   *Photo on page 5.*

Mix muffin batter only until ingredients are moistened; it will be lumpy.

2 cups Basic Baking Mix, page 121	**1 egg, beaten, or equivalent**
4 teaspoons sugar	**2/3 cup water or milk**

Grease 12 muffin cups. Preheat oven to 400F (205C). In a medium bowl, combine Basic Baking Mix and sugar. Stir egg into water or milk. Stir egg mixture into Mix and sugar. Stir about 15 strokes to blend. Spoon batter into prepared muffin cups, filling each cup about two-thirds full. Bake about 20 minutes until muffins are raised and browned. Makes 12 muffins.

Variations

Apple Muffins: Stir 3/4 cup finely diced, peeled apples, 1/4 teaspoon ground cinnamon and a pinch of ground nutmeg into dry ingredients.

Banana Muffins: Reduce water or milk to 1/2 cup. Combine with egg, 1/2 cup mashed banana and 1/4 teaspoon ground nutmeg before adding to Basic Baking Mix and sugar.

Orange Muffins: Substitute orange juice for water or milk. Add 1 teaspoon grated orange peel and 1 to 2 teaspoons sugar. Add 1/2 cup chopped walnuts or pecans, if desired.

Pecan-Caramel Muffins: Blend 1/2 cup packed brown sugar with 1/4 cup soft butter or margarine. Pat mixture evenly in bottom of 12 greased muffin cups. Place 1 or 2 pecan halves flat-side up in each cup. Spoon in batter as directed. Bake about 20 minutes in 375F (190C) oven.

Onion-Cheese Muffins: Add 2 tablespoons minced fresh onion and 1/2 cup shredded sharp Cheddar cheese or 1/2 cup Cheddar cheese powder to dry Basic Baking Mix.

Nina's Half & Half Bread

Introduce friends to the taste of whole-wheat with this bread.

7 cups hot water	**2-1/2 lbs. whole-wheat flour**
1/2 cup shortening	**(about 7-1/2 cups)**
1 tablespoon salt	**2-1/2 lbs. all-purpose flour**
1/2 cup sugar, honey or unsulfured molasses	**(about 8 cups)**
2 envelopes active dry yeast	
(2 tablespoons)	

In a very large bowl, combine water, shortening, salt and sugar, honey or molasses. Stir until shortening melts and water is warm. Sprinkle yeast over surface. Let stand 5 to 10 minutes until mixture is foamy. Add whole-wheat flour. Stir to combine, then beat thoroughly. Stir in enough all-purpose flour to make a medium-firm dough that is not sticky. Turn out onto a lightly floured surface. Cover and let rest 3 to 5 minutes. Clean and grease bowl. Knead dough until smooth and elastic, about 10 minutes. Place in prepared bowl, turning to grease all sides. Cover and let rise in a warm place until doubled in bulk. Grease five 9" x 5" loaf pans. Punch down dough. Divide into 5 portions. Shape into loaves. Place seam-side down in prepared pans. Cover and let rise in a warm place until rounded above pans, about 45 minutes. Preheat oven to 350F (175C). Bake 30 minutes until golden brown and loaves sound hollow when the bottoms are tapped with your fingers. Turn out of pans; cool on racks. Makes 5 loaves.

Spicy Beet Bread

Photo on pages 52 and 125.

Spread cream cheese on pink spicy bread for an afternoon treat.

4 cups all-purpose flour
1 teaspoon baking powder
1/2 teaspoon baking soda
1/2 teaspoon salt
2 teaspoons ground cinnamon
1/2 teaspoon ground cloves
1/2 teaspoon ground ginger

1 teaspoon grated lemon peel
2/3 cup vegetable shortening
1/2 cup granulated sugar
1 cup packed light brown sugar
2 eggs, beaten, or equivalent
1 (16-oz.) can cut beets
Beet Glaze, see below

Beet Glaze:
1/2 cup packed light brown sugar
1/4 cup orange juice

1/2 cup reserved beet liquid

Preheat oven to 325F (165C). Grease a 9" x 5" loaf pan; set aside. In a medium bowl, combine flour, baking powder, baking soda, salt, cinnamon, cloves, ginger and lemon peel. In a large bowl, combine shortening, granulated sugar and brown sugar. Add eggs. Beat until mixture is light and fluffy, about 4 minutes. Drain beets, reserving 1/2 cup liquid. Puree beets in a blender or food processor or by pressing through a fine sieve. Stir into egg mixture. Fold 3 cups flour mixture into beet mixture. Stir in 1/4 cup reserved beet liquid; reserve remaining beet liquid for glaze. Fold in remaining flour mixture. Spoon batter evenly into prepared pan. Bake about 50 minutes until a wooden pick inserted in center comes out clean. While bread bakes, prepare Beet Glaze; cover and keep warm. Place a rack over a piece of waxed paper on a flat surface. Remove baked bread from pan and place on rack. Pierce loaf several times with a wooden pick. Brush glaze over top of loaf. Serve warm or cold. Makes 1 loaf.

Beet Glaze:
In a small saucepan, combine brown sugar, orange juice and reserved beet liquid. Simmer over medium heat until mixture reaches 170F (75C) on a candy thermometer and is slightly thickened.

Buttermilk Corn Bread

Buttermilk adds a fresh flavor to corn bread.

1 cup Basic Baking Mix, page 121
1 cup yellow cornmeal
2 teaspoons sugar
1/2 teaspoon baking soda

1/2 teaspoon salt
1/4 cup buttermilk powder
1 egg, beaten, or equivalent
1 cup water

Grease an 8- or 9-inch-square baking pan. Preheat oven to 425F (220C). In a medium bowl, combine Basic Baking Mix, cornmeal, sugar, baking soda, salt and buttermilk powder. Stir egg into water. Add egg mixture to dry ingredients. Stir until dry ingredients are thoroughly moistened, but do not overmix. Pour into prepared baking pan. Bake 25 to 30 minutes until golden brown. Makes 6 to 8 servings.

How to Make Spicy Beet Bread

1/Stir pureed beets into egg mixture.

2/Pierce loaf several times with a wooden pick. Brush glaze over loaf.

Peggy's Whole-Wheat Bread

Make this large batch of bread for those who like a rich wheat flavor.

6 cups warm water
1/2 cup vegetable oil
1 tablespoon salt
1/2 cup honey

2 envelopes active dry yeast
  (2 tablespoons)
About 13 cups whole-wheat flour

In an extra large bowl, combine water, oil, salt, honey and yeast. Stir until yeast is softened. Let stand 10 to 15 minutes until mixture is foamy. Add about 8 cups flour. Stir to combine, then beat thoroughly. Stir in enough remaining flour to make a stiff dough. Turn out onto a lightly floured surface. Cover and let rest 3 to 5 minutes. Clean and grease bowl. Knead dough until smooth and elastic, about 10 minutes. Place in prepared bowl, turning to grease all sides. Cover and let rise in a warm place until almost doubled in bulk. Grease five or six 9" x 5" loaf pans. Punch down dough. Divide into 5 or 6 portions. Shape into loaves. Place seam-side down in prepared pans. Cover and let rise in a warm place until rounded above pans, about 1 hour. Preheat oven to 400F (205C). Bake loaves 10 minutes. Reduce heat to 300F (150C). Bake loaves 25 minutes longer or until loaves are browned and sound hollow when the bottoms are tapped with your fingers. Turn out of pans; cool on racks. Makes 5 or 6 loaves.

One of the favorite times for entertaining is before and during the holidays. With the help of a well-stocked cupboard, you'll have more time to spend in the company of friends. There will be no more need for frantic last-minute trips to the store. Plan ahead for your holiday shopping and you'll be prepared for everything from a small brunch to a large buffet dinner.

Before you stock up, consider The Magic Ten. Assuming you have a supply of spices, seasonings and leavening agents such as baking powder and yeast, you'll need only 10 additional foods for holiday baking and dining. These foods are flour, sugar, shortening, milk, eggs, butter or margarine, nuts, fruit, vegetables and a frozen turkey or a canned ham.

To avoid overloading your budget during the winter holidays, begin your shopping in September or even earlier. Before each shopping trip, add one of The Magic Ten to your list. For example, buy an extra bag of sugar. Don't open it until you're ready to begin holiday baking. Whenever you see eggs for less than you usually pay, buy the eggs instead of whatever other storage item you had on your list. Put them up in water glass, page 13. Depending on the number in your household and the amount of baking you usually do, stock up on 2 dozen to 5 dozen eggs.

Putting food by in this manner, your supplies will be shelved in less than 3 months and the cost will be hardly noticeable.

If you have fine crystal and silver packed away, unpack it and put everyone to work shining and polishing. A flurry of activity helps spread the holiday spirit.

Bright colors and appetizing aromas bring on a festive atmosphere. Include colorful candles and napkins in your purchases. Decorations often go on sale after the holidays. That's the best time to stock up for next year. When next year arrives, use your treasures to create a centerpiece. Add a few heirloom or homemade ornaments, paper flowers or miniature toys. The investment in these accessories will be minimal—the rewards will be maximum.

Gaily wrapped offerings from your kitchen will be most appreciated. Match up your friends to these enticing gifts: a decorative plate of assorted cookies, a basket of individual Apricot Gift Loaves, a jar of Mixed Fruit Chutney, a pot of Freezer Red Raspberry Jam and a container of Tantalizing Trail Mix.

Happy holidays!

Home for the Holidays

Madame Fournier's Tourtières

French-Canadian pork pie is a New Year's Eve favorite in New England.

2 lbs. ground pork
1 onion, chopped
1/8 teaspoon salt
2 to 2-1/2 tablespoons poultry seasoning
1 to 1-1/2 teaspoons ground allspice
1 cup warm water
2/3 cup milk

1 (1/2-oz.) pkg. butter-flavor granules
1/2 teaspoon salt
1 cup instant potato flakes
2 recipes Rich Pie Pastry for
    double-crust pie, page 113
About 2 teaspoons milk

Place ground pork and onion in a large heavy saucepan or pot over low heat. Cover and cook 1 hour, stirring frequently to break up pork and prevent sticking. Stir in 1/8 teaspoon salt, poultry seasoning and allspice. Remove from heat. Let cool. Combine water, milk, butter-flavor granules and 1/2 teaspoon salt in a large bowl. Add potato flakes and stir gently to mix well. Let stand 2 minutes. Fold potato mixture into pork mixture; set aside. Preheat oven to 375F (190C). Prepare Rich Pie Pastry. Divide pastry ball into 4 portions. Shape each portion into a ball, then pat each ball flat. Roll out 1 portion of dough on a generously floured surface to a 10-inch circle. Roll up over rolling pin and center over an 8-1/2-inch pie pan. Unroll dough circle from rolling pin, fitting it into pie pan. Fill lined pie pan with half the pork mixture. Roll out another dough ball and use rolling pin to place rolled out dough on top of pie. Flute edges to seal and decorate with a dough cutout. Attach cutout onto pastry with a little water. Use a knife to make several air vents in top crust. Repeat with remaining dough balls and pork mixture. Flute and decorate. Brush each pie with about 1 teaspoon milk. Bake 25 to 30 minutes until golden. Serve warm or cold. Makes two 8-1/2-inch pies.

Variation

Lucille Berry's Tourtières: Substitute 3 cups fine breadcrumbs for the potato flakes. Add 1 teaspoon ground nutmeg. Substitute 2 recipes Flaky Pie Pastry, page 113, for the Rich Pie Pastry.

Onion Sauté

Storing fresh onions is described on page 16.

1 large onion
2 tablespoons butter or margarine
1/2 teaspoon dried leaf basil

1 cup frozen peas, partially thawed
Salt

Slice onion and cut slices in half. Melt butter or margarine in a medium skillet over medium-low heat. Add onion and basil. Sauté over medium heat until onion is tender. Stir in peas. Cover and cook over low heat 5 minutes. Salt lightly. Serve immediately. Makes 4 servings.

Shown on the following pages, clockwise starting at the top: Christmas Wreath, page 141; Frozen Cranberry Salad, page 136; Cinderella's Pumpkin Pie, page 135; Roast Turkey, page 134; and Savory Stuffing, page 135.

Roast Turkey   *Photos on pages 132 and 133.*

Try this cloth method of roasting a turkey for your next holiday dinner.

1 (12-lb.) frozen turkey
Water
Savory Stuffing, opposite
1 to 2 tablespoons butter or margarine,
   room temperature

1/2 cup vegetable oil
Gravy, see below

Gravy:
2 tablespoons all-purpose flour
1 tablespoon cornstarch
6 tablespoons giblet cooking liquid
Juices from cooked turkey

1/2 teaspoon poultry seasoning
1/8 teaspoon pepper
1/4 teaspoon celery salt
1/4 teaspoon onion powder

Thaw turkey according to package directions. Remove giblets and neck. Boil in water to cover, 30 minutes to 1-1/2 hours. The longer giblets are cooked, the more flavorful the broth will be. Prepare Savory Stuffing using giblet cooking liquid for the broth. Stuff cavities at both ends of turkey. Secure openings with skewers and lace with kitchen twine. Spoon extra stuffing into a small casserole. Rub turkey all over with butter or margarine. Place in a roasting pan. Preheat oven to 425F (220C). Pour vegetable oil into a large bowl. Cut a piece of white cotton, muslin or linen cloth to a 20" x 14" rectangle. Drench cloth in oil, then place over turkey, **being sure ends of cloth are not hanging outside roasting pan**. Place turkey in preheated oven; reduce heat to 325F (165C). Roast 2 hours, lifting cloth and basting every hour. Reduce heat to 200F (95C). Roast 3 hours, continuing basting every hour or more often as desired. Place casserole with extra stuffing in oven for last hour of cooking time. Pierce thigh deeply with a fork. Turkey is done when juices run clear. Remove from oven. Remove and discard cloth. Place turkey on a platter. Cover with foil or roasting pan cover and let stand 20 to 30 minutes. Prepare Gravy. Remove twine and skewers from turkey before carving. Serve turkey with gravy. Refrigerate leftover turkey in a food-storage bag or wrapped in a damp cloth towel. Makes about 12 servings.

Gravy:
Mix flour, cornstarch and giblet cooking liquid in a small bowl. Blend until smooth. Heat turkey juices in roasting pan over medium heat until boiling. Turn off heat. When boiling stops, gradually add flour mixture, stirring constantly. Turn heat to low and bring mixture to a simmer. Stir in remaining ingredients. Cook over low heat 5 minutes, stirring occasionally. Add more giblet cooking liquid, if desired. Spoon fat from surface of gravy before serving.

Savory Stuffing

Photos on pages 132 and 133.

Mix the dry ingredients ahead to shorten preparation time on the big day.

6 to 8 white bread slices,
   lightly toasted
2 (1/2-oz.) pkgs. butter-flavor granules
1/3 cup dried chopped celery
1/3 cup dried minced onion
1 teaspoon ground rubbed sage
1 teaspoon ground thyme
1/2 teaspoon ground allspice
1/2 teaspoon ground savory
1-1/2 teaspoons grated orange peel

1/2 teaspoon salt
1/4 teaspoon pepper
5 prunes
2 to 3 tablespoons dry sherry or
   orange juice
1/2 (16-oz.) pkg. frozen sliced apples,
   partially thawed
3 cups chicken broth or
   giblet cooking liquid

Cut toasted bread into 1/2-inch cubes to make 6 cups bread cubes. Combine bread cubes, butter-flavor granules, celery, onion, sage, thyme, allspice, savory, orange peel, salt and pepper in a freezer bag or container. Store in freezer. When ready to stuff turkey, place bread mixture in a large bowl. Pit and dice prunes. Place in a small bowl and cover with sherry or orange juice. Cut partially frozen apple slices in half. Pour chicken broth or giblet cooking liquid over bread mixture; mix well. Stir in halved apple slices and prune mixture. Makes stuffing for one 12-pound turkey.

Cinderella's Pumpkin Pie

Photos on pages 132 and 133.

If your coach turns into a pumpkin you can always make it into a pie!

Flaky Pie Pastry for a double-crust pie,
   page 113
4 eggs, slightly beaten, or equivalent
1 cup sugar
1-1/4 teaspoons salt
1 tablespoon ground cinnamon
1/2 teaspoon ground ginger

1/4 teaspoon ground cloves
1/4 teaspoon ground allspice
2 (13-oz.) cans evaporated milk
1 teaspoon vanilla extract
1 (29-oz.) can pumpkin
Whipped Topping, page 118, if desired

Preheat oven to 400F (205C). Prepare Flaky Pie Pastry. Roll out dough and line two 9-inch pie pans following directions on page 113. Combine remaining ingredients in a large bowl; mix well. Pour pumpkin mixture into unbaked pie shells. Bake 15 minutes, then reduce heat to 350F (175C) and bake 45 minutes longer. Decorate with Whipped Topping, if desired. Makes two 9-inch pies.

If pastry browns too quickly while baking, cover it loosely with aluminum foil.

Sweet-Potato Custard

Nutmeg and orange peel give an original flavor to this sweet-potato dish.

2 eggs, slightly beaten, or equivalent
1/4 cup sugar
1/2 teaspoon salt
1/4 teaspoon ground nutmeg
1 teaspoon grated orange peel

1-3/4 cups milk
1 medium, sweet potato, peeled, shredded
   (2-1/2 cups)
1 tablespoon butter or margarine, melted

Butter a 12" x 7" baking pan; set aside. Preheat oven to 350F (175C). In a large bowl, combine eggs, sugar, salt, nutmeg, orange peel and milk. Add shredded sweet potato and butter or margarine. Stir to blend. Sweet potato should be shredded immediately before adding to the egg mixture so it won't darken. Pour into prepared pan. Bake about 30 minutes until custard is set. Makes 4 to 6 servings.

Variation

Substitute 1 (16-ounce) can sweet potatoes or yams, drained, for the fresh sweet potato. Cut canned sweet potatoes or yams into small cubes before adding to egg mixture.

Frozen Cranberry Salad   *Photo on pages 132 and 133.*

This eye-catching salad is always a great favorite with children.

4 cups frozen cranberries
2 to 3 large apples, peeled, cored
1 cup miniature marshmallows
1 cup sugar
1/2 teaspoon grated lemon peel,
   if desired

1 (1.25-oz.) pkg. whipped topping mix
1 cup cold milk
1/2 teaspoon vanilla extract
1/2 cup chopped walnuts
1 thinly sliced lemon or lime for garnish

Grind frozen cranberries with the coarse blade of a food grinder or thaw slightly and chop a few at a time in a blender or chop by hand. Grind or shred apples. In a large bowl, combine ground cranberries, ground or shredded apples, marshmallows and sugar. Stir in lemon peel, if desired. Let stand at least 2 hours or refrigerate overnight. Combine whipped topping mix, cold milk and vanilla in a deep bowl. Beat on high speed until soft peaks form, about 2 minutes. Continue beating until topping is light and fluffy, about 2 minutes longer. Fold whipped topping and walnuts into chilled cranberry mixture. Spoon mixture into a 13" x 9" baking pan. Cover tightly and store in freezer until solid or up to 2 months. To serve, let stand at room temperature 30 minutes. Cut into 2- to 2-1/2-inch squares. Arrange on a platter. Garnish with lemon or lime slices. Makes 12 to 15 servings.

How to Make Sweet-Potato Custard

1/Peel and shred sweet potato.

2/Add shredded sweet potato and butter or margarine to egg mixture.

New Year's Sandwich Loaf

Spread each bread layer with butter to prevent the filled loaf from getting soggy.

Pineapple-Ham Sandwich Spread, page 38
Tuna Sandwich Spread, page 38
Chicken-Bacon Sandwich Spread, page 38
1 (1-lb.) round bread loaf, unsliced
About 2 tablespoons butter or margarine

2 tablespoons pasteurized process
  cheese spread
1/2 (3-oz.) pkg. cream cheese, softened
Pimiento-stuffed olives, sliced

Prepare sandwich spreads. Refrigerate in covered containers until ready to use. Slice bread horizontally into 4 equal layers. Spread butter or margarine equally on each layer except top layer. Spread buttered side of each bread layer with one of the sandwich spreads. Place layers on top of each other. In a small bowl, beat cheese spread with cream cheese until blended. Spread on top of layered loaf. Garnish with olive slices. Wrap loosely in aluminum foil and refrigerate. Serve as soon as possible. To serve, unwrap and place on a bread board. Cut in half vertically then slice each half. Each sliced layer may be picked up in fingers for eating. Makes 8 to 10 servings.

Festive Ham   *Photo also on cover.*

Use leftover ham in Fried Rice, page 59.

1 (5-lb.) can fully cooked ham
1 (17-oz.) can apricot halves
in heavy syrup

1 cup apricot-pineapple preserves
1/2 cup raisins
20 to 30 whole cloves

Preheat oven to 350F (175F). Line a baking pan with aluminum foil. Place ham on a rack in lined baking pan. Bake 1 hour. Drain apricots, reserving 1/2 cup syrup in a small saucepan. Stir in preserves and raisins. Warm over low heat until preserves are melted. Place apricots in a single layer in a baking pan. Use a sharp knife to score top of ham in a diamond pattern. Insert a clove in the center of each diamond. Remove ham from rack and place in baking pan on top of apricots. Spoon raisin-fruit syrup evenly over ham and apricots. Bake 15 minutes. To serve, place ham on a platter. Arrange apricots around ham. Spoon syrup from baking pan over ham and apricots. Makes 12 to 14 servings.

Cranberry Soufflé

Cherry extract is also delicious in this soufflé.

3 egg whites or equivalent
3 tablespoons sugar
1/2 teaspoon strawberry extract
1/2 cup drained whole-cranberry sauce

Fluffy Strawberry Sauce, see below
12 to 15 whole cooked cranberries
for garnish

Fluffy Strawberry Sauce:
1 egg white or equivalent
Pinch of salt
1-1/2 cups powdered sugar, sifted
1/4 cup butter or margarine,
room temperature

1/2 cup light corn syrup
1/2 teaspoon strawberry extract

Lightly oil top part of a double boiler; set aside. In a medium bowl, beat egg whites until soft peaks form. Gradually beat in sugar until stiff but not dry. Beat in strawberry extract. Fold in cranberries. Spoon into prepared pan. Cover and place over hot water. Cook over low heat 1 hour. Prepare Fluffy Strawberry Sauce; cover and refrigerate. Warm a 6- or 8-inch serving plate. Remove pan cover and invert soufflé onto warm plate. Serve immediately. Cut with a sharp knife. Spoon sauce over each serving. Garnish each serving with 2 to 3 whole reserved cranberries. Makes 4 to 6 servings.

Fluffy Strawberry Sauce:
Beat egg white until fluffy. Add salt and beat until soft peaks form; set aside. Combine powdered sugar, butter or margarine, corn syrup and strawberry extract in a medium bowl. Beat until smooth. Gently fold in beaten egg white until no white can be seen. Makes about 2 cups.

Festive Ham

Mincemeat-Pear Pie

Stir a little brandy flavoring into the mincemeat for a warm holiday flavor.

1 (16-oz.) can sliced pears
  in heavy syrup
Water
1 (9-oz.) pkg. condensed mincemeat

Flaky Pastry or Rich Pie Pastry for
  double-crust pie, page 113
1 teaspoon grated lemon peel
About 2 teaspoons milk

Drain pears, reserving syrup. Add water to reserved syrup to make 1-1/2 cups liquid. Crumble condensed mincemeat into a medium saucepan. Add liquid mixture. Bring to a boil over medium heat, stirring frequently to break up lumps. Boil 1 minute to thicken mixture. Remove from heat; cool. Cut pear slices into bite-size pieces. Preheat oven to 425F (220C). Prepare pastry. Roll out dough and line a 9-inch pie pan following directions on page 113. Add cut-up pears and lemon peel to cooled mincemeat mixture; mix well. Turn into prepared crust. Cover with top crust. Trim and flute edges. Cut several slits in top of pie to let steam escape while baking. Brush pie with milk. Bake about 30 minutes until golden. Makes 8 servings.

Apricot Gift Loaves

The flavor becomes richer after they are refrigerated or frozen for a few days.

1 cup apricot preserves
2 cups all-purpose flour
1/2 cup whole-wheat flour
1/3 cup sugar
2 teaspoons baking powder
1/4 teaspoon salt
2 eggs, beaten, or equivalent

1 cup apricot nectar
1/2 cup instant milk powder
2 tablespoons vegetable oil
1/4 cup sugar
1/4 cup apricot nectar
2 tablespoons rum flavoring

Preheat oven to 350F (175C). Butter five 5-1/2-inch loaf pans. Melt preserves in a small saucepan over low heat. Sift together all-purpose flour, whole-wheat flour, 1/3 cup sugar, baking powder and salt into a large bowl. Beat eggs, 1 cup apricot nectar, milk powder and oil in a medium bowl. Pour into flour mixture. Add melted preserves and stir to combine. Divide batter between prepared pans. Bake 30 to 35 minutes or until a wooden pick inserted in center comes out clean. Cool cakes in pans on a rack. Combine 1/4 cup sugar and 1/4 cup apricot nectar in a small saucepan. Stir over low heat until sugar is dissolved. Stir in rum flavoring. Use a skewer to make several holes in each cooled loaf. Pour rum mixture equally over each loaf. Let stand 30 minutes. Remove cakes from pans and wrap individually in aluminum foil or plastic wrap. Refrigerate or freeze in freezer bags. Makes 5 small loaves.

Christmas Wreath   *Photo on pages 132 and 133.*

An especially impressive gift that's easy to make.

1/3 Holiday Sweet Bread dough, page 142
4 to 6 candied red cherries, cut in half
1/3 cup candied lemon peel or mixed
   candied fruits, if desired

1/4 cup granulated sugar
2 or 3 drops red or green food coloring
2 tablespoons butter or margarine, melted
Snowy Frosting, see below

Snowy Frosting:
1/2 cup powdered sugar
2 to 2-1/2 teaspoons milk

Butter a large baking sheet or 12-inch pizza pan. Divide dough in half. Pinch enough dough from each half to make four or five 1-inch balls of dough, making 8 to 10 balls altogether. Pull dough from sides of 1-inch balls to bottom and pinch together, making surface smooth and even. Arrange balls seam-side down in a circle on prepared baking sheet or pan, about 2-1/2 inches apart. Roll remaining 2 pieces of dough between your hands into ropes 3/4 to 1 inch thick and 30 to 36 inches long. Weave the 2 ropes around balls of dough. Cross ropes between balls, weaving them over and under one another. Pinch ends to seal. Adjust number of balls and length of ropes, if needed. Press your finger into top of each ball of dough. Insert 1 cherry half, rounded-side up, in each ball. Place pieces of candied peel or fruit on each side of balls of dough, if desired. In a small bowl, combine granulated sugar and red or green food coloring. Brush dough with melted butter or margarine. Sprinkle with colored sugar. Cover and let rise in a warm place until doubled in bulk. Preheat oven to 375F (190C). Bake wreath 25 to 30 minutes until golden brown and ropes sound hollow when the bottoms are tapped with your fingers. Cool on pan on a rack. Prepare Snowy Frosting. Drizzle frosting over cooled wreath. Makes 1 loaf.

Snowy Frosting:
In a small bowl, combine powdered sugar and enough milk to make a smooth frosting.

Recipes in this book calling for milk were tested with reconstituted instant-milk powder. Recipes requiring eggs were tested with reconstituted dried eggs, frozen eggs or eggs in water glass, page 13.

Poinsettia Coffeecake

Really say Christmas with this attractive coffeecake.

1/3 Holiday Sweet Bread dough, below
3 tablespoons butter or margarine, melted
2 tablespoons granulated sugar

1/2 cup mixed candied fruits and peels
  or finely chopped candied cherries
Snowy Frosting, page 141

Butter a large baking sheet or 18-inch pizza pan; set aside. Roll dough out to a 16" x 12" rectangle, about 1/4 inch thick. Brush melted butter or margarine over surface except for a 1/2-inch strip along 1 long side. In a small bowl, combine sugar and candied fruits and peels or chopped cherries. Arrange over buttered area. Roll dough jelly-roll-fashion from long buttered edge toward unbuttered edge. Pinch edge against roll to seal. Use a sharp knife to cut ends of roll on a diagonal. Place end pieces in center of prepared baking sheet or pan. Cut remaining dough in 1-inch diagonal slices. Dough will flatten slightly into pointed oval slices. Arrange slices cut-side down and touching in a circle around end pieces. Place slice so upper point is to the center and lower point is to outside. Cover and let rise in a warm place until doubled in bulk. Preheat oven to 350F (175C). Bake about 25 minutes until lightly browned. Cool on pan on a rack. Prepare Snowy Frosting. Drizzle frosting over cooled coffeecake. Makes 1 coffeecake.

Holiday Sweet Bread

A basic sweet dough for many festive holiday breads.

1/2 cup warm water
2 envelopes active dry yeast
  (2 tablespoons)
1/2 teaspoon granulated sugar
2 cups hot water
1 cup butter, margarine or shortening
1/2 cup granulated sugar, packed brown
  sugar or honey

1 teaspoon ground cinnamon
2 teaspoons grated lemon or lime peel
1/2 teaspoon ground nutmeg
2 teaspoons salt
3 eggs, beaten, or equivalent
2/3 cup instant milk powder
6 to 8 cups all-purpose or
  whole-wheat flour

In a small bowl, combine 1/2 cup warm water, yeast and 1/2 teaspoon granulated sugar. Let stand until foamy. In a large bowl, combine 2 cups hot water and butter, margarine or shortening, stirring until fat is melted. Stir in 1/2 cup sugar or honey, cinnamon, lemon or lime peel, nutmeg, salt, eggs and milk powder. Cool to warm. Stir in yeast mixture. Stir in about 3 cups flour. Beat 100 strokes by hand or 2-1/2 minutes by machine. Stir in enough remaining flour to make a stiff but tender dough. Turn out on a lightly floured surface. Let rest 5 minutes. Clean and grease bowl. Knead dough until smooth and elastic and small bubbles form under surface. Place in prepared bowl, turning to grease all sides. Cover and let rise in a warm place until doubled in bulk. Punch down dough. For a finer texture, let dough rest 30 minutes before shaping. Divide into 3 equal pieces. Shape into braids, rings, coffeecakes, Christmas trees or Christmas wreaths. Makes 3 or 4 large loaves.

How to Make Poinsettia Coffeecake

1/Arrange candied fruit and sugar over buttered area of dough.

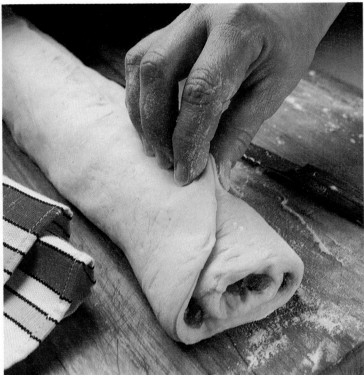

2/Roll up dough jelly-roll-fashion. Pinch edge against roll to seal.

3/Cut dough in 1-inch diagonal slices.

4/Arrange dough slices in a circle around 2 end pieces.

Steamed Christmas Pudding

Garnish the platter with a sprig of holly for a special touch.

Gingerbread batter, page 118
1 cup chopped nuts, if desired

1 cup chopped dates
Lemon Sauce, see below

Lemon Sauce:
1 cup powdered sugar, sifted
**1/3 cup butter or margarine,
    room temperature**

1/4 teaspoon lemon extract
3/4 teaspoon vanilla extract
Pinch of ground nutmeg

Generously butter a 3-cup fluted metal mold. Prepare Gingerbread batter. Fold in nuts, if desired, and dates; do not bake. Turn batter into prepared mold about two-thirds full. Cover tightly with foil. Place on a rack in a 4-quart pressure cooker. Pour water 3 inches deep in cooker. Adjust cover on cooker. Place over medium heat until steam flows from vent. Let steam flow 30 minutes. Set control at 5 pounds pressure. When control begins to jiggle, reduce heat. Control should occasionally jiggle, indicating steam is up to pressure. Cook 30 minutes after control jiggles. Prepare Lemon Sauce; set aside. Reduce heat on pressure cooker immediately by placing cooker under cool running water. When pressure control weight can be removed without a flow of steam, remove control and remove cover. Remove mold from cooker. Remove foil. Top of pudding will feel dry. Invert molded pudding onto a platter. Remove mold. To serve, cut pudding in wedges; place wedges on dessert plates. Top each serving with a generous tablespoon of Lemon Sauce. Makes 6 to 8 servings.

Lemon Sauce:

Beat powdered sugar 2 tablespoons at a time into butter or margarine. Stir in lemon extract, vanilla and nutmeg. Refrigerate only 15 minutes before serving.

Variation

If you do not have a pressure cooker, place covered mold in a deep pan. Pour water 3 inches deep around mold. Heat over medium-high heat until water comes to a boil. Reduce heat until water is barely simmering. Cover pan tightly. Simmer over low heat 2-1/2 to 3 hours. Add more water as necessary.

To make brown sugar, beat 1 to 2 tablespoons of molasses into each 1/2 cup of white granulated sugar. Measure the mixture before using it.

Independence Day Tartlets

Don't wait for a parade to display these irresistible miniature pastries!

Rich Pie Pastry for double-crust pie,
   page 113
Whipped Topping, page 118

1/2 (21-oz.) can cherry pie filling
1/2 (21-oz.) can blueberry pie filling

Prepare Rich Pie Pastry. Prepare Whipped Topping; refrigerate. Roll out pastry as if making a double-crust pie, page 113. Place 2-inch tartlet pans upside down on dough. Use a knife to cut around each pan. Press a dough cutout into each tartlet pan with your fingers, trimming edges if necessary. Prick bottom of each shell 3 times with a fork. Preheat oven to 450F (230C). Place pans with shells on baking sheets. Bake 8 to 10 minutes until golden. Remove from oven. Let cool slightly. Remove shells from pans and place on a plate or tray. Fill half the shells with cherry pie filling. Fill remaining shells with blueberry pie filling. Before serving, top each tartlet with Whipped Topping. Makes about 32 tartlets.

Variation

Campers' Tartlets: Substitute 12 to 16 individual graham cracker tart shells for the dough tartlet shells. Substitute 1 (21-ounce) can pie filling for the 2 half cans. Top filling with a mixture of 2 tablespoons shredded coconut and 2 tablespoons chopped walnuts.

Mixed Fruit Chutney   *Photos on pages 37 and 87.*

Surprise your friends with a gift of spicy East Indian relish.

1 (12-oz.) pkg. mixed dried fruit
1/2 cup raisins
2 tablespoons chopped candied fruit
1/2 cup water
1 cup white vinegar
1-1/2 cups sugar

3 whole cloves
1 (1-inch) piece of cinnamon stick
1/2 teaspoon garlic powder
1/2 teaspoon ground ginger
1/2 teaspoon ground coriander

Sterilize small jelly jars and lids according to manufacturer's instructions. Dice mixed dried fruit. Combine all ingredients in a medium saucepan. Bring to a boil over medium heat, stirring occasionally to dissolve sugar. Reduce heat, cover and simmer 45 minutes. Let cool. Spoon cooled chutney into small jars. Cover tightly. Label with contents and date. Chutney may be stored at room temperature for short periods or refrigerated for 1 year or longer. Makes 3 to 4 cups.

Who can resist the aroma and flavor of homemade candies or a plate of cookies? Stocking up on the basics for a family cookie bake or a candy-making party could be one of the smartest things you've ever done! Make a batch of cookies on a rainy day and invite a friend over. Brew a pot of herb tea or serve steaming mugs of hot cocoa. For a refreshing summer drink, combine a can of frozen orange juice concentrate and a can of frozen limeade concentrate. Add water or soda water and, if you like, vanilla ice cream. Set the table with pretty plates, napkins and a few flowers or a bit of greenery. Relax and enjoy the day!

One of the nicest gifts you can give a busy friend is an assortment of homemade cookies. Arrange them on a disposable brightly colored plate or on a reusable pie plate. Wrap the plate and cookies in plastic wrap. Then gift-wrap in tinted cellophane and top with a graceful bow. To begin your cookie gift project, bake cookies all year round and freeze each kind of cookie in a separate container with a tight-fitting lid. For short-term storage of 1 to 2 weeks, store in a cool pantry or cupboard. For longer storage, place the container in your freezer.

Cookies are wholesome treasures when they're packed in a school lunch. Add both fun and nutrition to your youngster's mid-day meal by including a few Wheat & Chip Cookies or Butterscotch-Oatmeal Cookies.

When you make Big-Batch Gingerbread Cookies, cut out part of the dough into gingerbread men. Use brightly colored ribbon to tie the gingerbread men to your Christmas tree for delightful edible decorations. You can also tuck them into the tops of Christmas stockings so early risers on Christmas morning will have a treat to munch on!

Store semisweet chocolate, butterscotch, carob and other flavored pieces in your refrigerator. They'll keep for months.

Seal or tightly cover opened packages or cans of nuts. Then store them in the freezer or refrigerator. For ease in handling frozen nuts, let them thaw 15 to 30 minutes at room temperature before chopping.

Neighborhood Cookie Bake

Chocolate Snow Caps

Marshmallow topping makes these cookies special.

5 tablespoons butter or margarine, room temperature	1/4 cup all-purpose flour
1/3 cup sugar	1/4 cup whole-wheat flour
1 egg, beaten, or equivalent	1/4 teaspoon salt
1/2 teaspoon vanilla extract	1/4 teaspoon baking powder
6 tablespoons unsweetened cocoa powder	1/2 cup chopped walnuts or pecans
	Marshmallow creme

Preheat oven to 350F (175C). Butter baking sheets. In a medium bowl, cream together butter or margarine, sugar, egg and vanilla. Combine remaining ingredients except marshmallow creme in a small bowl. Add cocoa powder mixture to creamed mixture; mix well. Drop batter from a teaspoon onto prepared baking sheets. Bake 10 minutes or until firm. Cool on a rack. To serve, spread top of each cooled cookie with marshmallow creme. Makes 25 to 30 cookies.

Fancy Filled Cookies   *Photo on page 151.*

Cookies soften as they absorb moisture from the filling and frosting.

1/2 cup butter, margarine or shortening
1/2 cup granulated sugar
1 teaspoon vanilla extract
1/2 teaspoon grated orange peel
2 tablespoons water
1-1/2 cups all-purpose flour

1/4 teaspoon baking powder
1/2 teaspoon salt
2 tablespoons buttermilk powder
Orange Frosting, see below
1 cup orange marmalade, or
   peach or apricot jam

Orange Frosting:
2 cups powdered sugar, sifted
1/4 cup butter or margarine,
   room temperature

2 to 4 tablespoons orange juice
1 tablespoon orange marmalade, or
   peach or apricot jam

Preheat oven to 375F (190C). In a medium bowl, cream together butter, margarine or shortening and granulated sugar until fluffy. Beat in vanilla, orange peel and water. In a small bowl, combine flour, baking powder, salt and buttermilk powder. Stir into creamed mixture until mixed well. Use your hands to shape mixture into 1-inch balls. Arrange on ungreased baking sheets. Depress centers with your fingertip or thumb. Bake about 10 minutes until lightly browned. Do not over-bake. Cool on racks. Prepare Orange Frosting. Spoon 1/4 to 1/2 teaspoon marmalade or jam into depressed center of each cooled cookie. Use about 1 teaspoon frosting to cover each cookie, sealing in marmalade or jam. Place filled cookies 1 layer deep in a flat container with a tight-fitting lid. Let them stand 1 or 2 days before serving. Makes 50 to 60 cookies.

Orange Frosting:
In a small bowl, combine powdered sugar, butter or margarine, orange juice and marmalade or jam.

Butterscotch-Oatmeal Cookies

These chewy cookies will become firm favorites.

3/4 cup shortening
3/4 cup butter or margarine,
   room temperature
1 cup packed brown sugar
1 cup granulated sugar
2 eggs, beaten, or equivalent

1/4 cup evaporated milk
1 teaspoon vanilla extract
1-3/4 cups all-purpose flour
3/4 teaspoon salt
1/2 teaspoon baking soda
3 cups rolled oats

Butter baking sheets. Preheat oven to 375F (190C). In a large bowl, beat shortening and butter or margarine until blended. Beat in brown sugar and granulated sugar until smooth. Add eggs, evaporated milk and vanilla. Beat until mixture is fluffy. Sift together flour, salt and baking soda into sugar mixture. Blend thoroughly. Stir in rolled oats. Drop batter from a teaspoon onto prepared baking sheets. Bake 10 to 12 minutes. Makes about 60 cookies.

Christmas Caramels

Wrap these in tinted cellophane and hang them on the Christmas tree.

2 cups sugar
Pinch of salt
1/2 cup buttermilk powder
1 cup light corn syrup
1/2 cup evaporated milk

1/2 cup water
2 tablespoons butter or margarine
1-1/2 teaspoons vanilla extract
1/4 cup chopped walnuts, if desired

Butter a 9" x 5" glass loaf dish; set aside. In a large saucepan, combine sugar, salt and buttermilk powder. Stir in corn syrup, milk and water. Stirring constantly, bring to a boil over medium heat. Stir occasionally on bottom and sides of pan below surface of mixture. Continue to boil gently until mixture reaches 115F (45C) on a candy thermometer. With a clean spoon, stir in butter or margarine. Over low heat, boil slowly about 1 hour until mixture reaches 240F (115C) or 28F to 30F above boiling water at your altitude, or firm-ball stage. Mixture will turn golden brown. Set aside without stirring. Cool to about 150F (65C) or very warm to touch. Stir in vanilla. Add walnuts, if desired. Pour candy into prepared dish. **Do not scrape sides of pan.** Cool to room temperature. Turn out on a cutting board. Use a sharp knife to cut candy into 3/4-inch squares. Run a table knife along either side of sharp knife to separate candy from knife. Wrap pieces individually in plastic wrap. Pack wrapped candies in freezer bags or containers with tight-fitting lids. Seal and store in refrigerator 2 weeks or in freezer 3 months. Makes about 72 candies.

Big-Batch Gingerbread Cookies

Children enjoy shaping cookies from this non-sticky dough.

1 cup unsulfured molasses
1 cup shortening
1 cup sugar
1 egg, beaten, or equivalent
1 teaspoon vanilla extract
6 cups all-purpose flour
1/2 teaspoon ground ginger

1 teaspoon salt
1/2 teaspoon ground cinnamon
1/4 teaspoon ground cloves
2 teaspoons baking soda
1/2 cup water
Red candies, raisins or colored decors

In a small saucepan, combine molasses and shortening. Bring to a rolling boil. Set aside to cool 10 minutes. In a large bowl, combine sugar, egg and vanilla, beating until creamy. Stir in cooled molasses mixture; set aside. Sift together flour, ginger, salt, cinnamon and cloves. Stir baking soda into water. Stir into molasses mixture alternately with flour mixture. Preheat oven to 375F (190C). Turn dough out on a lightly floured board. Pat or roll dough 1/8 inch thick. Cut in designs with cookie cutters. Using a metal spatula, carefully lift cut dough onto ungreased baking sheets. Decorate cookies with red candies, raisins or decors. Bake 10 minutes or until edges become firm. Do not overbake or cookies will be too crisp when they cool. Makes about 100 cookies.

How to Make Christmas Caramels

1/Add buttermilk powder to sugar and salt in a large saucepan.

2/Use a sharp knife to cut candy. Separate candy from sharp knife by inserting a table knife between candy and sharp knife.

Whole-Wheat Refrigerator Cookies

Just as delicious if you substitute all-purpose flour for part or all of the whole-wheat flour.

1-1/2 cups butter, margarine or
   shortening
3 cups packed brown sugar
3 eggs, beaten, or equivalent
5 cups whole-wheat flour

3/4 teaspoon salt
1-1/2 teaspoons baking soda
1 cup chopped walnuts or pecans,
   if desired

In a large bowl, cream together butter, margarine or shortening and brown sugar. Beat in eggs until mixture is fluffy. In a medium bowl, combine flour, salt and baking soda. Gradually stir into creamed mixture. Stir in chopped nuts, if desired. Shape dough into a roll about 13 inches long. Wrap in waxed paper or foil. Refrigerate at least 2 hours. Preheat oven to 425F (220C). Cut refrigerated dough into 1/4-inch slices. Arrange on ungreased baking sheets. Bake 8 minutes or until firm. Use a metal spatula to remove baked cookies from baking sheet. Cool on racks. Makes about 100 cookies.

Layered Bars

A sure winner.

Rich Milk, page 112
2-1/2 cups Easy Granola, page 23
1/2 cup butter or margarine
2 tablespoons sugar

1 cup shredded coconut
1/2 cup chopped walnuts or pecans
1 cup chocolate, butterscotch or
    peanut butter flavored morsels

Prepare Rich Milk; set aside. Prepare Easy Granola. Preheat oven to 350F (190C). In a 13" x 9" baking dish, melt butter or margarine in preheating oven. Stir granola and sugar into melted butter or margarine. Pat mixture evenly over bottom of baking dish. Bake 10 minutes. Spread coconut and nuts evenly over baked crust. Pour Rich Milk evenly over entire mixture, being sure to cover edges and corners. Bake 10 to 12 minutes or until set. Sprinkle with morsels. Let stand 5 minutes for morsels to soften. Use a small spatula to spread melted morsels evenly over surface. Let cool to room temperature before cutting. Makes 15 to 18 bars.

Hope's Peanut Butter Fudge

Buttermilk adds a creamy richness to the fudge.

3 cups sugar
1/4 cup cornstarch
1/4 cup buttermilk powder
1/4 teaspoon salt
1 cup evaporated milk

1/2 cup peanut butter
2 tablespoons butter or margarine
2 teaspoons vanilla extract
1/2 cup chopped walnuts, if desired
Peanuts for garnish, if desired

Lightly butter a 9-inch-square baking pan. In a medium saucepan, combine sugar, cornstarch, buttermilk powder and salt, stirring to blend. Stir in evaporated milk. Bring to a boil over medium heat, stirring constantly to prevent scorching. Continue to stir and boil gently 4-1/2 minutes; remove from heat. Stir in peanut butter and butter or margarine until both are melted. Stir in vanilla. Add walnuts, if desired. Beat with a wooden spoon until candy mounds when dropped from a spoon onto a plate. Quickly pour or spoon into prepared baking pan, spreading evenly. If desired, garnish with peanuts while fudge is soft. Let cool to room temperature before cutting. This candy freezes well or can be stored at room temperature or in the refrigerator. Makes about 50 pieces.

Starting at the top, Chocolate & Peanut Butter Chews, page 152; Hope's Peanut Butter Fudge; French Bonbons, page 152; Layered Bars; and Fancy Filled Cookies, page 147.

French Bonbons   *Photo on page 151.*

Get a head start on your holiday baking by making and freezing these in November.

1 cup finely chopped or ground dates	**1/4 teaspoon vanilla extract**
1/2 cup finely chopped or ground walnuts	**3 to 5 drops red food coloring,**
1/2 teaspoon vanilla extract	** if desired**
2 egg whites or equivalent	**5 to 7 drops green food coloring,**
Pinch of salt	** if desired**
2/3 cup sugar	

Lightly butter baking sheets or line baking sheets with brown paper. In a small bowl, combine dates, walnuts and 1/2 teaspoon vanilla. Shape into 1/2-inch balls; set aside. In a medium bowl, beat egg whites until frothy. Beat in salt, sugar and 1/4 teaspoon vanilla until stiff peaks form. Divide meringue equally in 2 small bowls. If desired, add red food coloring to 1 bowl and green food coloring to the other bowl. Stir gently until coloring is evenly distributed. Preheat oven to 250F (120C). On prepared baking sheets, spoon meringue mixtures 1/4 teaspoon at a time in mounds about 2-1/2 inches apart. Place a date-walnut ball on top of each mound. Spoon about 1 teaspoon of the same color meringue on top of each date-walnut ball. Use a metal spoon to smooth sides, sealing to meringue on bottom. Swirl tops into peaks. Bake about 30 minutes or until set. Remove from baking sheet or brown paper while warm. Cool on racks. Makes 50 to 60 bonbons.

Variations

Jim Jams: Omit dates, walnuts and 1/2 teaspoon vanilla extract. Use 1/2 teaspoon vanilla extract in meringue. Fold 1/2 cup finely chopped walnuts into meringue. Bake at 225F (105C) 40 to 50 minutes or until dry.

Surprise Balls: Prepare as for Jim Jams. Fold in 1/2 cup small chocolate pieces with chopped walnuts. Bake as for French Bonbons.

Chocolate & Peanut Butter Chews   *Photo on page 151.*

Two favorite flavors make double-good cookies!

1/2 cup butter or margarine	**2 rounded tablespoons peanut butter**
1/2 cup milk	**1 teaspoon vanilla extract**
1-1/2 cups sugar	**3-1/2 cups quick-cooking oats**
3 tablespoons unsweetened cocoa powder	

Combine butter or margarine, milk, sugar and cocoa powder in a medium saucepan. Bring to a boil over medium heat, stirring constantly. Remove from heat. Stir in peanut butter, vanilla and oats. Drop batter from a teaspoon onto ungreased baking sheets or waxed paper; let cool. Store cool cookies in airtight containers. Makes about 60 cookies.

How to Make French Bonbons

1/Place a date-walnut ball on top of each meringue mound.

2/Smooth meringue over each date-walnut ball, sealing sides to meringue on bottom.

Wheat & Chip Cookies

Rolled whole-wheat is much more chewy and absorbs more liquid than rolled oats.

1 cup shortening
3/4 cup packed brown sugar
3/4 cups granulated sugar
1 teaspoon salt
1 teaspoon baking soda
2 eggs, beaten, or equivalent

1 teaspoon vanilla extract
1-1/2 cups whole-wheat flour
1 to 2 cups rolled whole-wheat or
   2 to 3 cups rolled oats
1 (6-oz.) pkg. chocolate pieces or
   carob pieces

Butter baking sheets. Preheat oven to 375F (190C). In a large bowl, cream together shortening, brown sugar, granulated sugar, salt and baking soda until fluffy. Beat in eggs and vanilla until thoroughly combined. Stir in flour and rolled whole-wheat or rolled oats. Stir in chocolate or carob pieces. Drop batter from a teaspoon onto prepared baking sheets. Bake about 10 minutes until lightly browned. Cookies will puff up, then flatten during baking. Cool on racks. Makes about 45 cookies.

Diane's Brownies

Frosting the brownies while they are still hot guarantees a fudgy texture.

2-1/2 cups all-purpose flour
2 cups sugar
1 teaspoon salt
1 cup butter or margarine
1 cup water
1/4 cup unsweetened cocoa powder
1 teaspoon baking soda

2 tablespoons buttermilk powder
1/2 cup water
2 eggs, beaten, or equivalent
1 teaspoon vanilla extract
Chocolate Frosting, see below
1/4 cup chopped walnuts, if desired

Chocolate Frosting:
3 to 4 cups powdered sugar, sifted
1/2 cup butter or margarine
1/4 cup unsweetened cocoa powder

1/3 cup milk
1 teaspoon vanilla extract

Butter a 15-1/2" x 10-1/2" jelly-roll pan. Preheat oven to 350F (175C). Sift together flour, sugar and salt into a large bowl. In a medium saucepan, combine butter or margarine, 1 cup water and cocoa powder. Stir over medium heat until mixture comes to a boil. Stir into flour mixture until smooth. In a small bowl, stir baking soda into buttermilk powder. Gradually stir in 1/2 cup water until smooth. Immediately stir into flour mixture. Stir in eggs and vanilla. Beat until smooth. Pour evenly into prepared baking pan. Bake 25 to 30 minutes until a wooden pick inserted in center comes out clean. Prepare Chocolate Frosting during final 15 minutes of baking. Spoon frosting over hot brownies. Sprinkle evenly with chopped walnuts, if desired. Lightly press walnuts into frosting. Cool to room temperature before cutting. Makes 25 to 30 servings.

Chocolate Frosting:
Measure 3 cups powdered sugar into a large bowl. In a small saucepan, combine butter or margarine, cocoa powder and milk. Stir over medium heat until mixture comes to a boil. Stir into powdered sugar. Beat until smooth. Beat in vanilla. Frosting should be thick enough to coat the back of a spoon. If it is too thin, add more powdered sugar.

Packaged Foods
Leave foods in their original packages if at all possible. Instructions for preparing foods are often printed on the package. Place the packaged foods inside airtight containers. If you must remove foods from their packaging, cut off the instructions, wrap them in plastic wrap and keep them with the food.

Orange-Carrot Cookies

Frosted cookies are a favorite dessert or snack.

1 (16-oz.) can sliced carrots, drained
   (1 cup mashed)
3 tablespoons thawed frozen orange
   juice concentrate
3/4 cup vegetable shortening
1 cup sugar
1 teaspoon vanilla extract

1 egg, beaten, or equivalent
2 cups all-purpose flour
1 teaspoon baking powder
1/2 teaspoon salt
1/2 cup chopped walnuts, if desired
Orange Blossom Frosting, see below

Orange Blossom Frosting:
1 to 1-1/2 cups powdered sugar, sifted
2 tablespoons thawed frozen orange
   juice concentrate

1/2 teaspoon vanilla extract

Lightly butter baking sheets. Mash carrots in a small bowl. Stir in orange juice concentrate; set aside. Preheat oven to 375F (190C). In a large bowl, cream together shortening, sugar, vanilla and egg. Sift together flour, baking powder and salt into creamed mixture. Add walnuts, if desired. Stir mixture until combined. Mound batter by teaspoonfuls on prepared baking sheets. Bake 12 to 15 minutes or until golden brown. Cool slightly on racks. Prepare Orange Blossom Frosting. Spread about 1/2 teaspoon frosting over top of each warm cookie. Makes about 36 cookies.

Orange Blossom Frosting:
In a small bowl, combine 1 cup powdered sugar, orange juice concentrate and vanilla. Beat until smooth. Frosting should be thick enough to coat the back of a spoon. If it is too thin, add more powdered sugar.

Fudge Cookies   *Photo on page 5.*

Chewy chocolate cookies will disappear before you can put the cover on the cookie jar!

1 (12-oz.) pkg. semisweet
   chocolate pieces
1 (14-oz.) can sweetened condensed milk

1/4 cup butter or margarine
1-1/4 cups all-purpose flour
1/2 cup chopped walnuts or pecans

Butter baking sheets. Combine chocolate pieces, condensed milk and butter or margarine in a medium saucepan. Stir over very low heat or in a double boiler over simmering water until chocolate pieces are melted. Remove from heat. Preheat oven to 350F (175C). Stir flour and walnuts or pecans into chocolate mixture. Drop batter from a teaspoon onto prepared baking sheets. Bake 7 minutes or until firm. Remove cookies from baking sheets. Cool on wire racks before storing in airtight containers. Makes 60 to 75 cookies.

What To Store

Basic Storage Items lists foods that should be in your storage plan. These foods are all you need to prepare many wholesome dishes from recipes in this book.

To create interesting and well-rounded menus, your cupboard should contain most of the items listed in Herbs, Spices & Flavorings.

Some recipes require other foods than are given in these 2 lists. They are foods you can store and use regularly, but they are not considered basic to food storage.

Basic Storage Items

Bacon, page 7
Baking powder and baking soda
Beef
   canned: roast beef
   frozen: chuck roast, ground beef, round steak, stew-meat
Bread
   frozen
Broth or bouillon, beef and chicken
   canned: cubes or granules
   frozen: homemade
Butter or margarine, or both
   frozen
Butter-flavor granules
Cereal
   hot and cold
Cheese
   dried: Cheddar cheese powder
   frozen: Cheddar, Longhorn, Monterey Jack, mozzarella, Parmesan
   spread: pasteurized process cheese spread
Chicken
   canned: whole, chunked and ground
   frozen: whole, pieces
Cornmeal
Cornstarch
Eggs, pages 12 to 14
   frozen, dried, in water glass
Fish
   canned: jack mackerel, shrimp, tuna
   frozen: fillets, steaks
Flour
   all-purpose, whole-wheat
Fruit juices
   canned, frozen, powdered (vitamin C fortified)
Fruits
   canned: applesauce, apricots, mixed fruit, grapefruit, peaches, pears, pineapple, mandarin orange segments
   dried: mixed fruit, raisins
   frozen: apples, strawberries, raspberries, whole citrus

Ham
   canned: whole, chunked and ground
Honey
Jams and jellies
Legumes
   canned: pinto beans, kidney beans, garbanzo beans
   dried: black beans, black-eyed peas, Great Northern beans, kidney beans, lentils, pink beans, pinto beans, soybeans, split peas
Lemon or lime juice
Mayonnaise
Milk, page 15
Molasses
Mung beans for sprouting, page 8
Mustard
Nuts
   frozen: almonds, pecans, walnuts
   unshelled: almonds, peanuts, pecans, walnuts
   vacuum-packed: almonds, peanuts, pecans, walnuts
Onions, page 16
Pasta
   ditalini, elbows, fettucini, lasagne noodles, spaghetti
Peanut butter
Pearl barley
Popcorn
Pork
   frozen: chops, ground pork, pork loin, sausage
Potatoes, page 17
   canned, instant
Rice
   white long-grain, brown
Rolled oats and rolled wheat
Root cellar vegetables, page 4
Sugar, page 17
Sunflower seeds
Sweet relish
Tomato paste and tomato sauce
Vegetable oil and shortening
Vegetables
   canned: beets, carrots, corn, green chilies, green and yellow beans, zucchini, lima beans, mixed vegetables, potatoes, ripe olives, tomatoes, water chestnuts
   dried chopped: bell pepper, celery, mixed vegetables, onion
   frozen: broccoli, brussels sprouts, carrots, corn, pea pods, green beans, peas, lima beans, mixed vegetables, zucchini
Vinegar
   cider, white, wine
Wheat, pages 94 and 95
Yeast
   active dry
Yogurt, page 18

Herbs, Spices & Flavorings

Allspice, ground	Dijon-style mustard	Paprika
Basil, dried leaf	Dill weed, dried	Poultry seasoning
Bay leaves	Freeze-dried chives	Red (cayenne) pepper
Celery salt	Garlic: dried minced, powder, salt	Sage, ground rubbed
Chili powder	Ginger, ground	Seasoned salt
Cinnamon: ground, sticks	Hot pepper sauce	Soy sauce
Cloves: ground, whole	Marjoram: dried leaf, ground	Tarragon, dried leaf
Cocoa powder, unsweetened	Nutmeg, ground	Thyme: dried leaf, ground
Coriander, ground	Onion powder and onion salt	Turmeric, ground
Cumin, ground	Orange peel	Vanilla extract
Curry powder	Oregano: dried leaf, ground	Worcestershire sauce

Useful Addresses

Listed below are the major producers and/or distributors of dehydrated foods in the United States. They can tell you where to find distributors of their products in your locality.

Dehydrated and/or Dried Foods:
Beehive Products, Inc.
P.O. Box 9086
Van Nuyes, CA 91407

Food Storage Sales
Distributors of Perma-Pak
3999 So. Main Street
Salt Lake City, UT 84107

Grover Company
2111 So. Industrial Park Avenue
Tempe, AZ 85282

Intermountain Freeze Dried Foods
3025 Washington Blvd.
Odgen, UT 84401

Manna Food, Inc.
592 Gordon Baker Road
Willowdale, Ontario
Canada M2H 2W2

Neo Life Company of America
25000 Industrial Blvd.
Hayward, CA 94545

Rainy Day Foods, Inc.
P.O. Box 71
Provo, UT 84603

Ready Reserve
18467 Railroad Road
City of Industry, CA 91748

Saco Food, Inc.
Developers of Dried Buttermilk
Powder
6120 University Avenue
P.O. Box 5461
Madison, WI 53705

Sam-Andy Products, Inc.
1660 Chicago Avenue P-1
Riverside, CA 92507

Freeze-Dried Foods:
Eastern Food Storage
166 Cushing Hwy, Rt. 3A
Cohasset, MA 02025

Futurity Products
1704 Taylors Lane, Unit 6
Cinnaminson, NJ 08077

Graham, Inc.
5304 Kalanianaole Highway
Honolulu, HI 96821

Grover Company
2111 So. Industrial Park Avenue
Tempe, AZ 85282

Heritage Farms
P.O. Box 564
Norcross, GA 30091

Intermountain Freeze Dried Foods
3025 Washington Blvd.
Odgen, UT 84401

Oregon Freeze Dry Foods, Inc.
P.O. Box 1048
Albany, OR 97321

RS Distributors
20292 S.W. Birch Street
Santa Ana Heights, CA 92707

Tradewind Products
516 N.W. 12th Avenue
Portland, OR 97209

Zernia Company
P.O. Box 438
Anchorage, AK 99501

Grains, Nuts, Grain Mills and other Equipment:
Contact local hardware stores, department stores, grain mills and grain sales outlets. Or write to the following companies for catalogs or the names of local distributors of their products.

Arrowhead Mills
P.O. Box 866
Hereford, TX 79045

CC Grains
6749 Marginal Way South
Seattle, WA 98108-3497

Country Life Natural Foods
Oakhaven
Pullman, MI 49450

Eden Food, Inc.
701 Tecumseh
Clinton, MI 49236

Erewhon
3 East Street
Cambridge, MA 02141

Garden Way Country Kitchen
Catalog
Charlotte, VT 05445

Grover Company
2111 So. Industrial Park Avenue
Tempe, AZ 85282

Laurelbrook Foods, Inc.
P.O. Box 47
Bel Air, MD 21014
or
2319 Laurelbrook Street
Rawley, NC 17604

Lifestream
12411 Volcan Way
Richmond, B.C.
Canada V6V 1J7

Magic Mill, International
235 West 2nd South
Salt Lake City, UT 84101

Nelson & Sons, Inc.
P.O. Box 1296
Salt Lake City, UT 84110

R & R Mill Co., Inc.
45 West 1st North
Smithfield, UT 84335

Retsel Corp.
P.O. Box 47
McCammon, ID 83250

Walnut Acres Mill & Store
R.D. 1
Penns Creek, PA 17862

Walton Feed, Inc.
P.O. Box 307
Montpelier, ID 83254

Most state Extension Services, local government offices or agricultural offices have bulletins for local residents on gardening and home storage of foods. Two valuable free bulletins from the U.S. Department of Agriculture are Home and Garden Bulletins Number 119, *Storing Fruits and Vegetables* and Number 78, *Storing Perishable Foods in the Home.* Inquire at your county Extension office. Or send your requests on a postcard to USDA, Washington, D.C. 20250 or Consumer Information Center, Department B, Pueblo, CO 81009.

The Basic Baking Mix, page 121, and recipes using it, with the exception of the Large-Quantity Baking Mix, are revisions from Missouri Mix for Home Baking, University of Missouri, Columbia.

Index

Acknowledgements

The authors wish to express their appreciation to the following people for help with recipe testing: Edna Buchanan, Catherine Felix, Hope Latham, Michele Peterson and Harriet Smallwood.

They also want to give special thanks to Nina Greenhalgh for her many good ideas on using whole-wheat kernels and to Renee Woods and June Gibbs as consulting Home Economists.

8.416019217623